Unspoilt Heart

Elizabeth Gowdie

AuthorHouse™ UK Ltd.
500 Avebury Boulevard
Central Milton Keynes, MK9 2BE
www.authorhouse.co.uk
Phone: 08001974150

©2010 Elizabeth Gowdie. All rights reserved.

No part of this book may be reproduced, stored in a retrieval system, or transmitted by any means without the written permission of the author.

First published by AuthorHouse   6/16/2010

ISBN: 978-1-4520-3813-1 (sc)

This book is printed on acid-free paper.

In memory of my dearest uncle Neilly McGinley who still lives in all our hearts

Acknowledgements

I would like to thank all the friends who read the first draft of the book, Kate Winton, David Skellington, Bobby McCluckie, Mairi Archer and others. Their comments encouraged me to carry on. Thanks also to my daughters Kirstin and Sarah Anne, for their most helpful feedback on later drafts, and to Kristin's husband Andrew Laing for his helpful replies. I am also very grateful to the enthusiastic research and memorabilia contributed by Neilly's daughters my twin cousins Mary and Kathleen McGinley and Neilly's son Neil junior. The front cover was conceived and completed by my husband Ian Gowdie. His creative contribution is much appreciated, as is my son Mark's help with the graphics and printing of the book. For Neilly's youngest sister Patsy, my Mother, gratitude for all her memories which are crucial to the integrity of the book.

UNSPOILT HEART

Small Treasures

When I was a young child I spent a great deal of time at the home of my maternal Grandmother. I always felt safe there, curled up warmly before the safe sleepy hearth the bright fire leaping, the kind brass blinking, and the smell of home made soup seeping from the kitchen. Then always on shining clean Sundays after mass in the well polished house, all the chattering Grandchildren sliding on the well waxed floor. All the grownups sipping well stewed tea, munching sweet gossip, and swapping Sunday hats. The crumbs of grownup conversation caught in our curious children's ears.

I was often on my own at my Grandparent's house. As there were no toys or games to occupy me, I would amuse myself by exploring the contents of my Grandmother's large elaborately carved side board drawers. Ever patient, my Grandmother was happy to let me do this. Both drawers were packed with, what to me, seemed fascinating treasures. There were military buttons, medals, a soldier's record of service booklet with my Uncle Neilly's name on it. There was also old Victorian jewellery, old photographs, a silver pocket watch from times gone bye, and coins from different parts of the world. My favourite coins were the pretty mother of pearl Japanese coins. Although I asked my Grandmother about the history of the things I had found, she never gave any satisfactory answers. Indeed she seemed to have forgotten how any of the items even got there.

Very carefully I would lay all my treasure out, and invent my own stories around these objects. I imagined a beautiful young heroic man with long blonde Viking locks, and the clearest blue eyes, who travelled to far distant places to fight for good, and vanquish all evil. On his travels my handsome young hero would gather items to remind him of the brave deeds he had carried out, and more importantly, of the many people whose lives he had changed. Indeed in my mind's eye, I was one of these lucky people.

I was a young Japanese princess kept safely by her very rich and powerful parents in a fantastically beautiful castle. Inside this beautiful castle, life was quite wonderful. The little princess had every comfort imaginable. The very best food cooked by the very best cooks in the land, the most exquisitely beautiful clothes to wear, and the softest and finest bed linen to fall asleep on at night. Luxurious fruit, oranges, lemons, mangoes, pears, and peaches, hung from the branches of wonderful fragrant trees, begging to be eaten. Every thing was golden and beautiful.
The castle was surrounded by a large deep lake. Yet all around the lake were other forbidden fruits. Groups of laughing grubby children chased one an

other through the long wild grass, and wild untamed flowers. Their squeals of sheer delight, were music to her young ears, and the little princess longed to join them, on the banks of the lake, for despite her own majestic surroundings in the castle, she had never had any companions of her own age.

One day as she was watching the children at play, a tall young man with long fair hair, who was hauling a small boat into the water, called to her across the lake. "Would you like to play to?" The princess was delighted and declared that she would very much like that. The young stranger then rowed across the lake to fetch the princess and carry her to the shore. The princess had a truly most wonderful time with the children, and to reward the young man for his kindness, gave him three beautiful mother of pearl coins. The Japanese coins that were now in my Grandmother's side board drawer.

Also in my grandmother's side board drawer were the books. One in particular fascinated me. It was large and leather bound. The book depicted famous artists' paintings of the crucifixion of Christ. The paintings brought tears to my eyes, and I could not understand how anyone could inflict such pain and suffering on another person. I suppose I was a sensitive and dreamy child. Yet I was also an inquisitive child.

If I had not been an inquisitive child, I may never have rummaged through my Grandmother's sideboard drawers and found my Uncle's poem.

These simple sad few lines were folded between the pages of the leather bound book. I then, may never have had the desire, to one day, write this tribute to my Uncle. As a young child I did not fully realise the significance of all of the items I had found, but I tucked them away safely in the back of my mind, for another day.

Uncle Neilly's Poem

As I lie at night and ponder
 Over days not long gone by,
My sad thoughts often wander,
And moisture dims my eye,
As I count the vows so simple,
We made we would not part,
I can feel my throbbing temples,
Try to ease a sad sore heart.

Childhood days we spent together,
 Happy days I can recall,
As they say through stormy weather
Yes we both came through it all,
Together we joined the Argylls
When soldiering was fun,
Happy days among the heather,
Then home when war was done.

Then the fight for freedom,
Both in the kilted ranks
Wearing a kilt and a sporran,
Learning to charge at tanks,
Looking forward to beating the Jerries,
 And earning the Nation's thanks,
Volunteers for far Malaya,
Again we moved as one,
Full of love and life and laughter,
And hoping its halcyon.

Then the war in earnest
We had to separate,
After so long together,
Alone you met your fate,
If they had killed you with a bullet,
Or in glory you had fell,
I wouldn't feel so bad pal
But they made your life hell,
They worked and beat and starved you,
 Till you finally found rest,
In the care of someone kinder,
Whose ways are always best.

That's my only consolation,
To pray your happy now,
And maybe watching o'er me,
To help me keep my vow.

*You always tried when living
To play a straight clean game,
And pleasure found in teaching,
Young lads to do the same,
Just an ordinary laddie,
There are thousands more and yet,
As a pal I found no equal,
You are one I'll ne'er forget,
So tonight dear pal though far away,
You've journeyed over the hill,
Your spirit a monument,
For young lads to follow still.*

*No your not forgotten Shaney,
You never died in vain,
As a champ you're still remembered,
May God rest you D McShane.*

The Early Days

Duncan McShane was a POW during the 2nd World War. He and my uncle were imprisoned in Japanese prisoner of war camps in Thailand, Malaya and Singapore, and put to work on the infamous Burma Thailand railway known as death railway. Both young men came from the same small town of Helensburgh in Scotland. They had grown up together joined cycling and cross country running clubs, and were the very best of friends. Duncan did not survive the camps, and like thousands of others, died of malnutrition and dysentery. My uncle spent four years as a prisoner of war in the Far East. When the camp was finally liberated Neilly was barely clinging to life.

Both men joined the Argyll and Sutherland Highland Territorial Army before the start of the war. The attraction was the outdoor training and the planned camping trips to the Isle of Man and other new exciting places. When war broke out the territorial soldiers were the first to be called up for active service. Neilly's Father John who had experienced the horrors of battle in the First World War, tried to dissuade his son from going to war. "You're an Irish citizen, and you're not obliged to fight for this country" his Father argued. His words had no effect on his young son who already felt a deep commitment to the country where he earned his living. The Argylls had a brave tradition of being the first to face action, and the last to leave the battle scene. At the fall of Singapore this was indeed true. The Argylls were fiercely loyal and were prepared to fight and lay down their lives, not for their commanding officers or the reigning King, but for the Regiment. The Regiment was their family. The Regiment was everything. Neilly and Duncan volunteered for service in Malaya and vowed they would stay together and look out for one another always. Their regiment was sent overseas, and during the trip Neilly celebrated his 21st Birthday aboard the troop ship. Yet nothing they knew in those carefree days that in responding to the challenge before them, a cold clammy blanket was soon to settle over their boyhood spring. Yet hope like the sun always rises and in brave young hearts, hope was always rising.

Eventually their regiment the 2nd battalion of the Argyll and Sutherland Highlanders was sent to Malaya for Jungle training, then onwards to Singapore. The soldiers in this unit received the best training in Jungle warfare. Also learning how to find food, and survive in this alien environment. Lt- Col Ian Stewart had put his men through intensive training pushing himself, and the men to the very limits of endurance.

As a result the 2nd battalion Argylls were tougher and more prepared for harsh jungle warfare than other battalions in Malaya. They were also the most effective in their efforts to repel the land invasion by the Japanese Imperial Army.

My Grandparents received only one letter from Neilly, in which he complained, that time was going slowly. He and his comrades had seen no action. This was suddenly, and sharply to change. On the 17th of December 1941, before the fall of Singapore, whilst cycling on his own, between base camps to deliver a military message, Neilly was captured by the enemy, and held prisoner in Changi prison camp. The previous night at Titi Karangan in Malaya, the Argylls had been preparing to meet the advancing Japanese army. In the pitch black night and in the torrential monsoon rains the Argylls got into position for the conflict about to begin. At 10am the following morning, the battle commenced as an advance party of Japanese troops began to emerge from the Jungle, close to the road. It was sometime in the next few hours that Neilly a despatch rider was ambushed, and taken prisoner. A few months later after Singapore fell, his fellow Argylls were also captured and sent to the same camp. Changi was a huge camp now located on the site where the former British barracks had stood. Neilly and his young companions were soon to discover that cruelty and complete disregard for human life was now their reality, as Japanese prisoners of war. The accommodation should have housed a thousand men, yet more than forty thousand prisoners were kept there.

The fall of Singapore was master minded by the shrewd and highly intelligent Japanese General Tomoyuki Yamashita. Singapore had a complacent population who felt that an attack on the peninsula was unlikely. Any attack which might happen would be from the sea, and could easily be repelled. Unknown to the British, Yamashita had been planning an invasion for more than a year. His plan relied on speed and surprise, and absolute commitment from the troops under his command. In February 1942 the Japanese launched a diversity attack landing on Malayan beaches. The attack was meant to distract the British troops in Malaya. The main attack was launched at night during the monsoon season and came from the land not the sea. The Japanese army pushed down through neutral Thailand, and British held Malaya. Due to the size of the operation Yamashita needed his men to carry twice as much in their kit bags as was the normal practice. To achieve this, the men travelled on bicycles. Twelve thousand troops stormed down the peninsula, each man willing to fight to the death.

Arthur Percival was the General in command of the British regiments, and learning of the advancing invasion, deployed troops to blow up strategic bridges to try and halt the progress of the Japanese army. However the Japanese were relentless, using their own soldiers to hold up logs strapped together to form human bridges, over which the cyclist army crossed the rivers in their paths. Churchill the Prime Minister of the time was adamant that Malaya would not fall to the Japanese. The peninsula was a valuable asset to Britain producing rubber and tin, and had to be defended. The Japanese troops used to fighting in tropical environments were appropriately kitted out in uniforms which protected them from the harsh jungle conditions. The allied troops sent to repel the invaders in contrast wore only kaki shorts, and short sleeved kaki shirts. Their exposed flesh was torn by the sharp thorny vegetation, and bitten by the jungle's multitudes of stinging insects. Thousands of British and allied troops were killed by the advancing Japanese. Many died in the most horrific and barbaric ways. Yamashita did nothing to dissuade his men from their actions. Only wounded men who could still walk were taken prisoner. The rest were executed in cold blood in front of their comrades. At the end of the war General Tomoyuki Yamashita was tried and executed for allowing his troops to commit these terrible war crimes.

General Percival now had no option but to withdraw his remaining troops to Singapore.

Thousands of allied soldiers had fled into the depths of the jungle to escape the carnage. Thankfully Neilly now a prisoner in Chungi camp did not have to experience this carnage. For his nightmare had not yet truly begun. The Japanese were also attacking Singapore from the air, bombing water and fuel pipelines and air strips. Food was running out. Civilians in panic were leaving in boats, and soldiers were deserting in their thousands. The battle was lost and General Arthur Percival had no choice but to surrender. The two Generals met, and the allies surrender accepted. Arthur Percival spent the rest of the war as a VIP prisoner of the Japanese. Arthur survived the war returning home to live out the rest of his life in quiet obscurity.

In Changi prison camp Neilly listened in fear and awe as the Japanese air attacks bombarded the area. His mind was spinning as he wondered how his unit was faring, and if his pal Duncan was still alive. Then day by day groups of allied soldiers began to arrive at the camp. To Neilly's immense relief Duncan was among them. In this tense and volatile situation both young men found security, and a little stability, in their happy reunion.

The men were not long in camp when word came that the Argylls were to leave for Thailand. Each man was given two fist size balls of cooked rice and allowed to fill his water bottle. Then heavily guarded they were taken to the railway station. When their train finally shunted in to the station, the Japanese pushed and shoved the men into the small, stifling metal box cars. The doors were barred, and the train slowly steamed off. The long cramped and torturous journey took five days. There was no room to lie down or sit properly. During the day the metal cars became unbearably hot, and at night were cold and wet with condensation. Smoke and soot seeped through the wagons making it hard to breathe. Mile after weary mile the train chugged on through Northern Malaya. As the rail road was single track, throughout the journey the train would frequently stop, and sit for hours in the searing hot sun, to let on coming trains pass.

Also travelling on this painful trip was Ernest Gordon one of the Argyll's company commanders. After the capture of Singapore in February 1942, the Japanese had ordered all the allied troops to surrender. Ernest and a few other officers had not obeyed this order, and had instead, purchased a fishing boat and tried to make their escape by sea to the safety of Ceylon. On the last lap of the escape bid they were spotted by a Japanese gun ship, and were forced to surrender. Others including Neilly's Cousin Scrapper had retreated into the Jungle to try and escape capture.

Chungkai

After a harrowing five days the men finally reached their destination at a place called Banpong. The men flooded out of the train to view their new home. The camp at Banpong made their previous accommodation at Changi look in comparison like a comfortable hotel. It was no more than a paddy field filled with huts. Inside the huts the bed platforms were barely three inches above the water. The latrines were overflowing and the smell of raw sewage caught in the men's throats. Neilly's heart sank. They had been promised better camps better food and better living conditions and naively they had believed their Japanese captors.

Ernest Gordon was eventually sent to a camp called Chungkai where prisoners were to put to work building the bridge over the River Kwai Chungkai initially was a base camp for a string of similar camps spread along the river. Eventually becoming a camp for the sick and dying. It was during this time that Ernest contracted diphtheria which almost took his life. It was only the kindness of other prisoners, and his own determination, that enabled the commander to survive. Two men in particular gave the officer the most dedicated care. Another officer known as Dinty, and Private Miller nick named Dusty, supported and nursed Ernest, until the worst of the illness passed. Both were deeply religious men. Dinty was a Roman Catholic, and Dusty a Methodist. Sadly neither Dinty nor Dusty survived their time in the camps. The gentle Christian and patient Dusty met the worst fate. Dusty had been sent to another camp where his quiet faith and goodness had infuriated the Japanese camp commander, who constantly taunted and tormented this beautiful man whose spirit he could not break. Finally in a fit of rage ordered Dusty's death in the most ignominious manner. The brave young Dusty met a slow and painful death. Dusty was crucified on a tree, as was his beloved Jesus. Although Dusty did not survive the war his goodness and gentle courage in the camps helped many other young men keep hope alive. For then he was as Jerusalem's lamb on slaughtered wood, whose martyred life, left life for men unborn to live.

Though life was short and suffered death was painful, his selfless love and clearest life were ever never wasted.

Before his death Dusty had helped establish a church in Chungkai camp where men of all faiths came together to pray and comfort one another. The church was simply a clearing in the jungle yet it sustained the spirits of the men who attended, and helped drive away the awful despair which hung in their hearts.

Missing in action

After his capture in Malaya there was no further news about Neilly or his regiment. Throughout the war .my grandmother never gave up hope, and attended all the Red Cross POW information meetings, in the hope that someone might have news about her only son. However, it was to be six months after the war had ended, before she learned Neilly was indeed still alive.

We now know that there were 14000 white prisoners in Japanese war camps. One in three died of starvation or disease. Those who endured the worst conditions were those who were sent to build the Burma Thailand railway. The project was inspired by the need to improve communications, and maintain the huge Japanese army in Burma and ultimately to invade India. Two groups of POW's one based in Thailand, and one in Burma, worked from opposite ends of the line towards the centre. The men had to construct the line which passed over rugged mountainous terrain, and through dense tropical jungles, in one of the most inhospitable climates on earth. In those camps from hell the men who endured this had to learn new things. Things they did not want to learn, in ways they did not want to learn them.

Toiling on the railway

Neilly and the rest of the captured regiment found themselves at the Thai end of the line. Their camp was encircled with barbed wire, and high wooden fencing. The huts the prisoners slept in were constructed from bamboo. A shaped frames were bound together with strips of tree bark. The roofs and sides of the huts were made from bamboo leaves overlapped like tiles, and kept out most of the rain. The cook huts were built with mud banks where huge woks could be placed over fire holes. Latrines were trenches with bamboo poles laid across for men to sit or squat on. Large covers were used to cover the cess pits, as they were infested with maggots. The flies produced from the maggots were everywhere in the camp, and the men had to constantly fan their food while they were eating.

Although their accommodation was dreadful Neilly and his colleagues soon learned that any thought of escape was pointless. Those who tried, were beaten and tortured, or executed in front of the whole camp, usually by beheading with the traditional Japanese sword. Very few of the Japanese guards spoke English and Neilly and his companions had also quickly to learn Japanese, in order to understand the commands, they were given. Failure to respond to a command, always earned a severe beating. Tenko was the daily roll call, when all prisoners had to call out their names in Japanese. The terms of the Geneva Convention were not adhered to by the camp commanders in charge.

Scrapper

There was one man who did manage to avoid capture when most of his regiment were imprisoned. Neilly's first cousin Scrapper / Neil Sharkey and two other men escaped into the Malaysian jungle. Scrapper was a tough man with a fierce heart. A strikingly handsome man, well over 6 ft in height afraid of nothing, and with the most penetrating and angry dark eyes. Unbelievably this imposing man managed to survive for more than a year in that harsh and treacherous jungle environment, while Neilly and the others were slaving on the railway. Scrapper's diet in the jungle was even more frugal than the P.O.W. in the camps. He fed on the bananas peppers and pumpkins which grew wild in the jungle, and sometimes managed to trap small mammals, which he roasted and ate. However there was no real escape. There was no place to go. In the end starvation forced Scrapper to return to the camp, sadly without his companions who had perished long before.

When he finally joined the others in the camp Scrapper was a terrifying sight. His long matted tangled hair and a thick beard hid most of his face. His eyes black as coal were sunken in his head. Crazed and staring, he raved and swore at the camp guards. Swaying on his bruised and bleeding feet, and waving long bony arms in the air he taunted his captors. "Come on then, you nip bastards. Take my head. Take my fucking mad head!" Scrapper then fell to his knees straightened his long thin frame and bowed his head for the blow of the sword. The blow did not fall.

The Japanese guards who had witnessed Scrapper's dramatic entry shrank in fear and horror from this terrifying spectacle. They were truly terrified of the ranting mad man, they now were looking at. The cruel little men scrambled and stumbled, and ran away from the ferocious Scrapper Sharkey. The Japanese were afraid of any kind of mental illness and thought that Scrapper was mad. Realising the effect he was having on the guards Scrapper was delighted and took to staggering about trying to chase the frightened little Japanese men, at the same time howling and roaring like a wild beast. The rest of the prisoners watching the drama, now saw the desperate humour in this weird situation, and began to laugh. The laughing became louder and louder. There was little opportunity for laughter for the men, and they made the best of it. The men shouted and jeered at the terrified Japanese, and cheered the actions of the wonderful Scrapper.

For the rest of his time in the camp Scrapper had no threat from any of his captors, who avoided any contact with him, and his angry black eyes. That amazing fearless man survived the war to return home, and live out some happy years with his wife and two daughters.

Neilly, Scrapper, and their companions housed in flimsy bamboo thatched huts continued to survive on food rations that were totally inadequate. Often supplies arriving at the camp were so long in transit, that they were contaminated and rotten. Neilly and the other POW often had to survive for weeks, on a small daily portion of rice, flavoured with salt. Red Cross parcels when the Japanese chose to distribute them, did help.

Jungle trips

I do remember that one of Neilly's comrades on his return home, told of how Neilly found a way of slipping out of the camp at night, and would run furiously to the nearest local village, and exchange red cross parcels for food, and much needed simple herbal medicines for other prisoners. His return to camp was just as fast a dash, as he needed to be back at the camp before his absence was discovered by the guards on patrol duty. This reckless bravery won Neilly the respect, and admiration of his fellow soldiers. It also earned Neilly cruel retribution when he was caught by the guards returning from one of these trips.

Neillys' punishment happened the following day. At dawn he was hauled from his hut and taken out into the centre of the camp. His thumbs were bound together with thin wire. He was then made to kneel on sharp stones and gravel. The excess wire which bound his thumbs was used to hoist Neillys' arms over his head where the wire was attached to a line above. Neilly was left in this agonising position in the scorching heat of the Thai sun for forty eight hours. To increase this torture the Japanese guards left a bucket of water in front of him. As the hours dragged on, fear and despair gripped Neilly's heart, and he felt he would not survive the terrible ordeal. Over the pain of the days Neilly tried to put himself in another more pleasant place, and some verses of an old poem spun in his head.

Mount Errigal looks over the Rosses so grand
The Atlantic roars oe'r the silvery sand
Hear the fifes and the drums of the Mullaghduff band
Down by Old Mullaghduf down by Mullaghderg strand

When his arms were eventually freed Neilly slumped to the ground. The skin on his head and body had been scorched by the searing heat of the sun. His arms were heavy and dead. Every bone in his body screamed in pain, and hot blood seeped from the dozens of stone puncture wounds in his knees and shins. The wire which had bound Neilly's thumbs had cut through to the bone. Neilly was unable to work on the railway for many weeks, man power lost through the actions of his captors. This was not the only time Neilly was tortured by his Japanese captors. On another occasion when Neilly was again caught returning from a trip out of the camp, when the Korean and Japanese guards brutally beat him with bamboo poles. Then he was made to squat inside a tiny stone structure, with a corrugated tin roof. These torturous devices were known as ovens. Over the course of the day the scorching sun would beat down on the tin roof, and the temperature inside made the unfortunate prisoner feel as if he was being cooked alive. Neilly was kept in one of these hellish contraptions for forty eight hours. One of Neilly's favourite songs was "Keep right on to the end of the road" and I am sure that thinking of the words of this stirring song may have sustained his soul, and spirit, and given him the courage to carry on.

Keep right on to the end of the road; keep right on to the end
Though the way be long and your heart beat strong keep right on round the bend
Though you're tired and weary still journey on 'til you come to your happy abode
Then all you love, that you are dreaming of will be there at the end of the road

Neilly and others made many similar dangerous trips and the medical team who were working with minimal supplies of medicine and equipment greatly appreciated any useful items the men were able to procure from the Thai villagers. Neilly was also indebted to the villagers who risked their own lives dealing with him, and on many occasions hiding him from Japanese patrols.

Sharing the blame

In later life Neilly also told his son Neil and Neil's wife Patricia when they were sitting in the garden at the Rhu house of another incident when he was subjected to torture. One morning after roll call David Boyle Neilly's commanding officer approached Neilly and told him that the Japanese had a head count the previous evening and had found two men were missing. In the morning when they assembled all the men all were present and correct. It was made clear to the prisoners that unless someone owned up to the offence of the previous night, all the sick prisoners in the medical hut would be carried on their stretchers out to the main camp and left to lie under the scorching sun. Neilly's company commander pleaded with Neilly to own up and take the punishment. Neilly protested as he had not left the camp that previous night, instead he had been spending time with his cousin Scrapper, and his friend Shaney. Duncan Mac Shane had also suffered dreadfully at the hands of the camp guards. He had been brutally beaten on too many occasions by a particularly sadistic guard. His jangled nerves were making him unable to sleep. Neilly had been trying to comfort and calm his dearest friend. It was common practice in the Argylls for every man to have a "mucker" That was a pal or friend they shared every thing with. Duncan and Neilly were the closest of "muckers" They had vowed to look after one another when they joined the Argylls. Duncan now needed him badly, and Neilly, was most reluctant to risk his life being tortured yet again. "They nearly killed me the last time I was tortured!" he said. "Get the ones who were out to own up" added Neilly. "I've already spoken to the men who were out, and they are refusing. If I don't get two volunteers the guards will carry out their threat, and lots of the lads are in such a bad way that they would have little chance of survival pleaded the commander. "I'm prepared to volunteer. I don't think they would want a dead senior British officer on their hands, so the punishment might not be too severe." replied the officer. Captain Boyle was persuasive, appealing to Neilly's good heartedness.

Eventually an agreement was reached, to avoid the sick men being left out in the burning sun, both Neilly and his commanding officer took the blame for the incident in question. As had happened to Neilly before, happened again to both men. Each had their thumbs bound together, their arms hoisted above their heads, and they were made to kneel on sharp gravel in the searing heat of the jungle sun. The Japanese were less harsh on prisoners who were officers. Officers also did not have to take part in manual labour and because of that, Neilly's punishment was shortened to twenty four hours instead of forty eight.

Hard labour

Life was unremittingly hard in the camp. Prisoners had to work from sunrise to sunset ten days on and one day off, moving earth, blasting through rock, and laying rail track. These harsh punishing conditions together with malnutrition and unsanitary living conditions caused Neilly to succumb to frequent bouts of malaria, and dysentery. Other prisoners suffered the horrific symptoms of beri beri. Beri beri was caused by a severe lack of vitamin B in the diet. Men's limbs would swell. They would lose feeling in their hands and feet. If left untreated this would lead to congestion of the lungs and eventually death by heart failure. Yet given the proper nutrition sufferers could make remarkable recoveries. A man's life could be saved by giving him the right type of food. Bartering with the native people for fruit and eggs saved many prisoners. Many P.O.W. fell ill with dengue fever caused by the bite of mosquitoes which carried the disease. There was no cure for this condition, only rest and lots of fluids. Despite their poor condition as long as they could walk the prisoners were expected to work.

The men had to push through dense jungle felling trees with only saws and axes. They worked while they lasted. It was genocide in the most cost effective way. Dead men did not have to be fed. Until then, they made themselves useful to the glorious Imperial

Japanese Army. It was ingrained in the Japanese culture that soldiers would fight to the death for their Emperor and country. Failure and capture by the enemy was not an option. Every Japanese soldier was prepared to commit suicide rather than fall into the hands of the enemy. They could not understand why the POW continued to struggle to live. They despised the men they had enslaved, and this made it easier for them to commit the terrible atrocities against them.

Nevertheless the imprisoned men did struggle hard to survive. They were inventive using rice sacks for bedding, and also for shrouds in which the dead were buried. Empty tin cans served as drinking vessels, and banana leaves as plates from which they ate their small rations of food. When their boots wore out they cut up old tyres and tied these to their feet with strips cut from the rice sacks. As their clothes turned to tatters and dropped from their backs, many could salvage only enough cloth to make themselves loin clothes. Yet many lost all hope, their bodies weak and frail, and their young hearts struggling so hard to beat, laid down their sad sorry heads, and surrendered their futures forever.

Childhood memories

It is hard to imagine that anyone could have endured all of this, and still survived, to be the Uncle I remember so fondly. The uncle who never lost his love of life. This small red haired man with eyes as blue as the summer sky, and heart as big as a bear, treated everyone he met, with open kindness, and respect, no matter what their position in life. Most of all Neilly loved children.

Closing my eyes with ease I climb back into my childhood and Neilly's home in Stucklekie Road Kirkmichael Helensburgh. I am seven years old, and playing with the twins. Kathleen and Mary the little blonde two year olds whom I adored and when they had grown to sixteen were bridesmaids at my wedding.
Neilly's family has reached six and would continue to grow. We are all playing tag in the garden. Aunt Rita throws up the sash window, and calls to us. She serves bags of home made chips through the window. Those chips taste like mana from heaven to us hungry kids.

Now the unforgettable family summer picnics are in my mind. Picnics by the side of the Fruin River. On a fine sunny day we would all set out on the uphill three mile walk to Glen Fruin, just north of our home town of Helensburgh. Aunt Mary and her four girls Annie with her brood of four. Me mum dad and both my younger brothers. Aunt Gracie, Uncle Jack, and their boy Owen. Neilly and Rita, with their tribe, now grown to seven or eight. Then Aunt Sadie and uncle Paddy who had no children of their own, yet loved all of us children most dearly.Our noisy happy group, pushed on with prams and pushchairs loaded up with provisions. Cutlery, plates, cups, pots and pans for cooking, and sausages, potatoes, tea, milk, cheese, bread, and fizzy lemonade.

When we arrived after our long walk Neilly would place the milk and lemonade to cool in the clear cool shallow waters of the River Fruin. The kids would gather twigs and wood from the forest, and Neilly would light the fire on which our meal would be cooked. The day was long and wonderful. Children squealing, laughing, splashing, and swimming in the sparkling cold waters of the Fruin River. Then Neilly would lead the band of children in single file into to the forest, snaking their way through the bracken, in search of an adventure. There we might catch a glimpse of a young red deer, or a flash of a fox in the forest.

The journey back home was not so exciting for us children now tired and grumpy, and Neilly would keep our spirits up by getting us to march along to a stirring rendition of "I love to go a wandering along the mountain track" Rita's favourite marching song was "It's a long way to Tipperary" and she would also lead our group of tired, but happy people on the march homewards.

NEILLY'S SON NEIL'S MEMORIES OF THOSE HAPPY TIMES

Faulderee Across the Fruin

After Mass on Sunday
Intae Friels for lemonade
Then we'd pack the sandwiches in the pram
Along wae scones that Mammy made
 Remember babies bottles
Extra nappies just in case
We'd all be goin a picnic
And Glen Fruin- Wis the place!

Fauderee Fauldera... wae a knapsack on my back

Some would walk and some would run
And some went in the pram
You had to watch oot for the wasps
If you ate a piece and jam
We'd pick up cousins on the way
Campbells, Smiths and Neils
All the way across the Fruin
You would hear the laughs and squeals!

Fauderee Fauldera... wae a knapsack on my back

At Walker's Rest we get a drink
From the wee hole in the wall

Our Granda used to work there
And he came from Donegal
The Big Ones used tae run ahead
And hide way oot o' sight
Then jump out from the bushes
And give the Wee Ones all a fright!!

Fauderee Fauldera... wae a knapsack on my back

We would gather wood
We would make a fire
On the fire, Faither cooked the food
Then boiled the tea up in a can
It always tasted good
We'd boil up the kettle
 Baked totties in their skin
Nothing tasted better
Than Goblin Burgers in a tin!

Fauderee Fauldera... wae a knapsack on my back
We take our trunks - wrapped up in towels
Faither wore big long khaki shorts
Gather up the docken leaves
They are a cure for stings and warts
We'd all climb up on Faither's back
Each of us in turn
Dad wis like a paddle steamer
Swimmin up and doon the Burn!!

*Fauderee Fauldera... wae a knapsack
on my back*

*When the day was over
It wis time ta pack oor bags
The Big yins turned tae wee yins
Tae get a Coaly Bag
I think the Faither's back is hurtin yet
We must have weighed a load
We must have looked like Tinkers
As we all marched doon the road!!*

*Fauderee Fauldera... wae a knapsack
on my back*

*Those Days across the Fruin
Are days we won't forget
Faulderee across the Fruin
I can hear it yet
Glen Fruin it holds memories
Happy memories for us all
It's our fondest childhood memory
Apart from Donegal*

*Fauderee Fauldera... wae a knapsack
on my back*

*Neil
May 1994*

Holidays in Ireland

Our family originated in Ireland indeed Neilly was born there. Some of my sweetest memories of my uncle Neilly were the family holidays, in the tiny village of Mullaghduff, on the far North West coast of Donegal. At least every other year we would holiday in this tiny crofting community, on that wild and beautiful coast. The worst part of the holiday was the journey over. None of the families were wealthy, and the cheapest mode of travel, was steerage by ferry boat across the Irish Sea, docking at London Derry harbour, and travelling to county Donegal over the border by bus. The ferry was also used to transport livestock in the winter months. In the summertime the animal quarters were cleaned out, and those on a tight budget could travel in these areas. The crossing was often in very rough seas, and I was always violently sick. Sick also on the road journey, to our part of Eire. However the long and unpleasant trip was always worthwhile, as the times spent in Mullaghduff, were the happiest and the funniest of my childhood.

One year I particularly remember, and still smile when it comes into my thoughts. Arriving in the early afternoon, on a beautiful cloudless summer day, my uncle Neilly took my brothers and me, with his boys to Mullaghderg beach. As we climbed over the rise of the sand dunes, the majestic sweep of the flawless sands, and dancing clear green blue water, was suddenly in view. Filled with exhilaration and the pure joy of youth, we all ran down the beach, and still fully clothed straight into the great Atlantic waves.

Neilly's good friend known as Tosh had also been a POW in Thailand. Tosh and Neilly had met in the camps. Tosh was a Birmingham lad whose regiment was the Leicestershires, had often accompanied Neilly on his trips out of camp to barter with local villagers for much needed supplies.

One year Tosh joined us on a family holiday in Mullaghduff. Tosh had attended Neilly and Rita's wedding and I remember him as a good natured man always with a ready smile. After the War Tosh would visit Helensburgh every year bringing greatly appreciated small games books and gifts for Neilly and Rita's expanding family. Tosh, an AA Rescue Patrolman married later in life and only had one daughter Diane, who was born blind and with some learning difficulties. My Mother Patsy had Tosh's daughter when she was a teenager, for holidays at our home in Helensburgh. Tosh's wife was not in good health, and his young daughter was at this time a challenge to care for. Mum felt life was difficult for Tosh and it was her way of trying to give him a break. Sadly Tosh died in 1975. He had been suffering from lung cancer and diabetes. Neilly and Rita travelled to Birmingham for the funeral of their very dear friend

We spent many days by the sea, happy as the day was long, running over ragged rocks, and swimming like little fishes in the cold Atlantic sea. Out of the sea we shivered and chittered, then laid our little skinny child bodies, on the soft sand, to be warmed by the heat of the sun.

Our childhood holidays in Ireland continued. In later times when we children were beginning to grow up a little, and looking for even more excitement, there were the midnight excursions to picnic on the same beach. Bare foot and walking over warm stones, the silver sands sighing softly in the dark, cooling from the day, and the long sea green grasses, swaying softly in the dark.

Back home in Helensburgh Neilly and his family were an important part of all our lives. When I was thirteen years of age My Mother lost her Father John. She was desolate as was my Grandmother, who now hated sleeping alone in her large flat. As space in my own home was tight, and I was still sharing a bed room with my two brothers, I moved in with my Grandmother. Both homes were close to one another and after tea I would go to her house and sleep over. I enjoyed my stay and this arrangement lasted on and off for almost seven years. Although it was a large flat with four bedrooms I slept in my Grandmother's room. I remember it was always best to get to bed well ahead of my Grandmother. For if I was too late in bed Granny's nightly prayer ritual would keep me awake for ages and ages! Granny would lay on her back the rosary beads in her hands, resting on her ample tummy and recite in a loud whisper all the decades of the rosary.

On Sunday nights after Benediction which was a service held at the nearby chapel Neilly and some of his older boys would visit the house. I greatly looked forward to these evenings when my cousins Johnnie, Michael, Neil, Gerry and I, would all have fun playing cards games while my Grandmother cooked the very best frying steak for Neilly. She, perhaps trying to make up, for those days in the camp, when Neilly existed on starvation rations.

I loved my time spent at my grandmother's, and shared it at times with my cousin Mary Ann when we were both teenagers. Mary Ann had been decanted from her home for the same reason as I was. Space was too tight in her family home. A few months after I married my husband Ian Gowdie I went to visit my Grandmother. I was at that time staying in a small flat in Scotstown Glasgow. I had just become pregnant with my first child, and was feeling so sick, that I was unable to attend teacher training college for four months. Granny was unwell and been in bed for a week with Flu. When I went into her bedroom to see her, I found her very down in health and spirits. Nothing I said could convince her that she would recover her health. She asked me to fetch her some soda water. When I returned she spoke to me very seriously, making me promise that when she passed away, I must remember to tell my Mother that her hand bag was under the bed. I thought that Granny's bag might hold a keepsake she wanted my mother to have, and tried to reassure my Grandmother that she would feel better soon.

Early next morning my lovely Grandmother Mary McGinley did indeed pass away. Most of her family were with her at the end. Aunt Sadie came quickly to fetch my Mother and I. We rushed out arriving at the house sobbing and panting for breath.

The house was now packed with grieving and tearful, young and old family members. Many taking turns going quietly in to say their last goodbyes to Granny. I was so shocked and quite unable to believe she was so quickly gone, that I could not enter the bedroom where she lay. I did however remember to tell my Mother where Granny's hand bag was hidden. When Mum found and opened the bag she gasped aloud and her shoulder's shook as she fought to control her tears, for inside the bag was enough money to pay for my Grandmother's funeral. Not wanting to be a financial burden on any of her family she had managed to save from her very small pension, enough money to pay for her own funeral expenses. How long this took we had no idea. It was a most caring and unselfish thing for my Grandmother to do. That was my Granny quiet and kind, thoughtful and unselfish. I missed her so very much, and it hurt me deeply that she did not live to see my first child Kirstin, who was born about five months later.

Dreaming of happier days

In the night as he lay on the floor of the bamboo hut, in the stifling clawing heat, listening to the sighs and groans of his exhausted sick companions, the most unbearable of all of these, was the sound of grown men calling for their mothers. Then Neilly's thoughts often turned to Ireland, to Mullaghduff his birth place, and he vowed he would return there if he survived the war. His happy boyhood days with Duncan now seemed like the tall sea house flashes, a blade of light seen swiftly, in this length of crushing darkness.

Then the soothing words of the old poem came in to his mind.

It was here that my forefathers lived long ago
And my love of this town land forever it grows
Nothing warms my heart more than to walk on the sand
Down by Old Mullaghduff down by Mullaghderg strand

Mullaghduff in the Rosses, North West Donegal
Ceud Mile Failte there's a welcome for all
Down by Old Mullaghduff down by Mullaghderg strand

The loss of Duncan

Dysentery had taken hold in the camp, and men were dying daily from this highly infectious illness which could be picked up from any surface that a sick man had touched. The men had no way of keeping their huts hygienically clean, and in their weakened condition they quickly succumbed to the disease. Duncan desperate to avoid the illness became obsessive about keeping his drinking cup clean, using precious drinking water to wash and re-wash the cup. It was heartbreaking for Neilly to watch his friend, a skeletal figure, weak and frail, and terrified of dying. Despite all efforts dysentery took him, as it did many hundreds of others in the camp. It was not a gentle death. Duncan raved and screamed. Tooth and nail he clung to life. Yet just before the new day dawned the light began to fade from Duncan's eyes. His clear eyes now clouded saw the world slowly sliding, while his young heart beat lastly, and his weary young body slipped back to the earth. When the light in his young friend's eyes left him, Neilly was left lonely without him. Tears streaming down his grief stricken face Neilly cradled Duncan's' head and rocked his friend's still warm dead body, as a mother would rock her child. Sitting beside his lifeless friend a paralysing calmness with a soft thud, draped it's self over Neilly's exhausted frame. All thoughts and feelings were emptied from him. The unseen air seemed to breathe all around him, and his mind flowed back to an evening in May, now a life time away, when there was love and light and laughter and two young lads were camping on the bonnie banks of a beautiful Scottish Loch.

Scrapper who was also in the hut nudged Neilly back to the pull of the clock, for soon it would be roll call, and if Duncan was not swiftly buried, their friends body would have to lie where it lay until the work party returned in the evening , after working on the rail track. Then Neilly and Scrapper had the sad and awful task, of burying Duncan's body. It was the practice to use rice sacks to encase the bodies of dead POW before burial. There were no other materials available. One sack was pulled over the upper body and another over the lower half. The dead prisoner was then buried in the earth and a cross made from bamboo was placed by the grave. A stone with the dead man's name regiment and date of his death scratched on to the surface was also added.

Duncan's death in that camp from hell almost broke Neilly. He lost his will to carry on. Yet other men loved him, and especially Neilly's cousin Scrapper who refused to let him give up. He and another prisoner known as Tosh spent every spare moment with Neilly trying to rally him round. Scrapper at the morning roll call would stare at the cruel little Japanese and Korean guards with his black dark eyes, and make his penetrating eyes swivel and cross. This visibly unnerved and disturbed the guards, and made the prisoners struggle to hide their mirth. In another camp, a Japanese guard while visiting the latrines, had been killed and eaten by a tiger. This news had travelled through the rail track camps, and struck fear in the hearts of all the camp guards. Scrapper had perfected an imitation of a tiger's ferocious roar, and would often out of sight from the guards, roar and growl like the beast they were all so afraid of. On hearing these terrifying noises, the Japanese soldiers although willing to die for their Emperor, would be thrown into a state of panic, for none wished to lose their lives to the jaws of a tiger. After the death of Duncan Neilly thought he would never laugh again, yet he to, battled with himself, and his shoulders shook, as he tried like the others to conceal his amusement, at the antics of his incorrigible but brave cousin.

Hell on earth

In a nearby camp cholera was rife, and the Japanese were terrified that it would spread to this camp. Overnight in the cholera stricken camp the men's huts filled with the dead and dying. The Japanese withdrew to a safe distance outside the camp, after barricading the entrance with rolls of razor wire and a large construction barrier in the shape of an X. Once you have lived through a cholera epidemic in a Japanese prisoner of war camp Hell holds no fear as you have already been there. To try and stop the disease from spreading, prisoners were not allowed to bury their dead. Instead the dead had to be burned. Those still alive had to make large funeral pyres with the bodies of their friends and companions. The fires had to be manned twenty four hours a day. It was particularly distressing for the men to witness the corpses of the men they knew, suddenly rise from the flames and jerk to a sitting position. One prisoner who joined Neilly's camp told of how one man who sat up from this human bonfire was still alive. A camp guard picked up a shovel smashed it down on the man's head and pushed him back into the fire. The POW who witnessed this horrific act was completely convinced that, even if he survived the war nothing would ever obliterate this dreadful memory from his mind.

Death in the most terrible way had become a daily part of the men's existence on death railway. It was not just the POW who had to endure this abominable cruelty, the local Asian people if caught trying to aid the POW in any manner, were put to death in the most inhuman ways. Other prisoners who had been in different camps had their own horror stories to tell. One man told of his experience, when an old Thai lady who worked in his camp smuggled a chicken out of the cookhouse. She threw the stolen chicken to a group of emaciated prisoners. However her sympathy for the starving men and her brave act of kindness was to cost her life. This kind old woman spotted by the guards was strung up by her wrists to a tree in that camp, and left with no food or water in the boiling hot sun until she finally died. The POW in that camp each morning before they set out for work on the railway, were made to stand before the dying woman to share in her pain. Three days later she was dead.

Neilly survived to continue the work on the railway. He had lost his dearest friend, and friends were vital in the camps. No one could survive without friends to look out for you, to help you when you were tired or sick. Yet there were times when even the loyalist friends, were not enough to keep men alive.

Speedo Speedo

As Neillys' work party moved further North, work on the railway became harder and harder. A granite like ridge butted up to the river. Teams of men worked in pairs using heavy sledge hammers and chisels to forge one metre holes in the rock. Other groups cut teak logs which were then dragged to the river, to build a viaduct by the rock ledge.

The exhausted prisoners were forced to work ten days on, and one day off. Their Japanese task masters drove the men on and on. They had somehow picked up the word "Speedo!" and would stand over the exhausted prisoners with their bamboo poles shouting "Speedo! Speedo!" and using the canes to beat any poor unfortunate souls they thought were not working fast enough.

Some men too weak from overwork sickness and starvation could not take the beatings and simply slid to the ground and died. When it rained the banks became slippery, and the men struggled to keep their balance. Humidity was high in the jungle and at midday temperatures often soared to 40 degrees. After a long days work the exhausted men trudged on foot back to camp, where they quickly fell into a deep sleep of oblivion. In the first morning light, as the men awoke, their sore eyes saw again the sharp slashing green Jungle cutting and stinging, and stamping it's dominance over them. Yet it was a reminder, that they were indeed still alive. The jungle was their tormentor. It was also beautiful to them. As they were roused from their sleeping racks they were born again. Just as the coming of air stone and water in the friction of compounds had created the first cell, and life for the men began to begin again.

In these moments Neilly thought that his Japanese captors would never truly conquer his spirit. For those front ranked hearts in the battle of dark, for a longer light lasting, were quite unable to hear in the ear of their longing, the snake's rattled warning. The ambitious Japanese had backed all their hopes on the straw of tomorrow, for a win that would wash their own war wounded hearts, and suspend them forever, at the peak of their hopes. Yet Neilly knew this would never be realised and somehow the goodness of other men would prevent this.

Bare foot saviour

During the monsoon weather men were still expected to work. In this non stop tropical rain heavy tree trunks had to be dragged through the mud, making the work doubly hard. White lice, scorpions and tropical sores all added to the misery of the men, who were by now a pitiful sight. It was in this torrential tropical rain that Neilly lost his footing, and fell from the viaduct around thirty feet into the river below, ripping his leg from thigh to ankle on a bamboo pole during his fall. Some of the guards on the river bank dragged Neilly from the water. Neillys' injury was horrendous. He was losing blood quickly. The guards shook their heads he was unlikely to survive they thought, and shrugging their shoulders, left Neilly in agony lying on the river bank. As it would soon be dusk, the order was given to return to camp. The guards did not care whether Neilly lived or died. He was of no use to them now and in the morning the other prisoners could bury what was left of him, after the beasts of the forest had had their fill of him.

One prisoner, who had witnessed the fall, did not return with the others. Owenie Burke a Glasgow man whose tough upbringing in that harsh city of the nineteen twenties and thirties, had equipped him with a fierce fighting spirit, together with an empathy for fellow suffering human beings, was Neilly's friend in need on that day. Owenie was a short stalky man stronger than average, and even now had more flesh on his bones, than most of the other men in the camp. When the guards disappeared Owenie scrambled down the river bank. Seeing Neilly's wound, tore up the remnants of his own tattered shirt, and bound together the edges of the gaping wound as tightly as possible. Then heaving Neilly on his back, he slowly made the exhausting climb back up the river bank. Reaching the top he rested for a few minutes to catch his breath, before setting off with Neilly on his back, for the long two mile painful walk back to camp.

Every bare foot step of the journey was agony for Owenie. Pain seared through every muscle and sinew and seemed to set his whole body on fire. The man on his back through groans of agony begged Owenie to set him down, and leave him behind. Owenie did as he asked, but only for a few moments to rest and ease his aching limbs. Their journey in the moonlight continued long into the night. Owenie shuffled over the rough jungle path carrying his human burden, only stopping briefly, to gasp for breath. Their two mile trip took almost two hours, and when they finally reached the camp, both men were soaked in Neilly's blood.

The kindness of others

Back at the camp most of the men were in their usual sleep of exhaustion. Those still awake, came out of their huts and were happy to see Neilly still alive. Neilly was loved and respected by his comrades and they now worked hard to help save his life. No anaesthetics were available, and Neilly's leg wound was sewn up without any pain relief. The wound was on the inside of Neilly's leg and damage extended to one testicle. The medic attending warned Neilly that if he survived the war he may have trouble fathering children. At this point in time nothing could have been further from Neilly's mind. The medical hut did have some bandages, and there were always maggots on hand to treat the wound should it fester.

During the next few weeks the men in the camp used part of their own meagre food rations, to supplement Neilly's diet and aid his recovery. The sick in the camps were put on half the normal meagre rations. The men had to supplement the diet of the sick in any way they could. The rats that ran over them at night were caught in home made traps, roasted and eaten. Neilly thought their white flesh tasted better than rabbit, a dish he was very fond of back home.

Even the maggots in the cess pits were used to keep men alive. One man had noticed that the chickens which fed on the maggots were becoming fat, and thought if this was good for the chickens it would also be good for the sick men. Bucket loads of maggots were hauled out of the pits carefully washed cooked and served with a sauce to Neilly and the other sick and injured men in the hut. These extra portions of protein visibly improved the men's health, and undoubtedly saved many lives.

Neilly was grateful for the kind attention of all the men. Grateful also that his pain was so much less than that of the men who had to have limbs amputated with makeshift surgical tools and no anaesthetic. Most lost legs through the complications caused by tropical ulcers. These poor souls were the most desolate of all, as the lay on their palettes unable to move around. Neilly was so saddened by their piteous condition that he spent as much time as he was able, chatting to the amputees about their lives and families back home. Neilly made a point of getting to know many of these men. Other good souls used their wit and imagination to fashion artificial legs for the sufferers, out of bamboo and metal cans. Neilly's company commander also tried his utmost to improve the life of the other men, organising a team of fairly fit men to regularly visit the sick and the low in spirit to comfort and help. The team also became proficient at massaging the limbs of men weakened by illness who had lost the ability to walk. This improved the circulation and the muscle tone of the sick men, most of who then learned to walk again.

Neilly and Owenie became firm friends. Their friendship was to last more than thirty years, and although neither man knew it at that time, they were also to become family as well as friends.

Neilly's injury eventually healed, and he once more returned to toiling on the railway.

Completion of the railway

The railway was finally completed on October the 17th 1943 at Konkuita in Thailand where the two sides met. The railway was 415 km long with a height difference of 300 meters. It included cross overs and bridges, of which one was the bridge over the River Kwai, and had been constructed in just 16 months. Engineer's original estimates had been five years. In total the labour force included around 68,000 allied POWs and 200,000 Asian labourers. The total death toll was around 96,000 human beings.

With the railway completed Neilly was now part of a team of maintenance workers, who moved up and down the track, making repairs to the tracks, bridges, and embankments. Ownie Burke was sent with another group, to dig caves into the hillsides. Huge cavities were blasted out of the mountain sides. The men were told that the caves were to serve as storage areas for military equipment. It was later established that the caves would serve as mass graves, where surviving prisoners would be incinerated, should the Japanese lose the war. However fate favoured these men, and because of the atom bombs the Japanese abandoned their plan to exterminate the surviving prisoners. Neilly and Owenie were not to meet again until some time after the war. Until this point neither knew if the other had survived.

The Bomb

However Neillys' health was deteriorating. Recurrent bouts of malaria, overwork and malnutrition had left his immune system shattered. In the medical hut all around him was oppressive damp heat, the smell of rotting flesh, and the moans of dying men. He had developed pneumonia and was close to death. On August the15th 1945 the bomb happened. Neilly had been in the medical hut for some weeks, drifting in and out of consciousness. Sometimes hallucinating about the hellish events he had witnessed and other times dreaming more gently, of his boyhood days on the shores of Mullaghduff, in County Donegal.
Despite his own suffering at the hands of the Japanese Neilly never changed his opinion about the dropping of these nuclear weapons. He felt the sacrifice too great. He also felt that the death of such high numbers of women and children was immoral, and should never have happened.

The Irish connection

Neilly often still dreamt of his home in Scotland, of his parents and sisters, especially his youngest sister Patsy the red haired teenager whose determined will and fiery temper exhausted his aging parents. Patsy had been born when Neillys father was in his fifties. How far into his fifties no one in Scotland quite knew, as John McGinley was a proud man who had married

Mary Sharkey, when she was just eighteen, and he being much more mature in years was not truthful about his own age. The absence of a birth certificate, which was destroyed during a Black and Tan raid on John McGinley's home village of Mullaghduff, only strengthened the idea, that he was indeed only a few years older than his teenage bride. The Black and Tans were mainly former British soldiers who had fought in the 1914-1918 First World War. Most returned home to find little prospect of employment. Few employers wished to hire men whose main skill was fighting in war. Many had experienced trench warfare and were still suffering the traumatic effects of this. When the government advertised for men who were willing to face a rough and dangerous task, many former British soldiers replied to the advert. The pay at ten shillings a day was a strong incentive to these unemployed ex-service men. Three months training was given and they were sent to Ireland. Their task was to subdue the activities of the Irish Republican Army, the I.R.A.

The pursuit of Independence from Britain had dominated Ireland during the late 19th century and the early 20th century. After the 1916 Easter uprising when armed Irish nationalists organised a rebellion against the British rule in Ireland many of their leaders were executed. Public opinion was outraged, and the Rebels cause was greatly strengthened. The Black and Tans lacked self discipline and in their quest to combat the Irish rebel activities, terrorised the local people. The Black and Tan troops found it impossible to defeat the Irish men who were using guerrilla warfare against them. Ordinary Irish people living in areas where the I.R.A. was suspected of having a base suffered at the hands of the Black and Tan soldiers. Those in rural areas suffered most. In my Grandfather John McGinley's small village of Mullaghduff, the invaders swept through the tiny village and burnt the inhabitant's modest homes to the ground. .The local church was also burned. The villagers of the time lost all records of Births Deaths and Marriages in the fires. It was then that my Grandfather's Birth certificate was destroyed. The Black and Tans earned their nickname because of the mixture of uniform they wore. As there were not enough British military uniforms to serve all the men, these were mixed with the uniforms of the Royal Irish Constabulary. This mixture of khaki and dark police uniform gave rise to the name Black and Tans. However the Black and Tans achieved nothing in Ireland, they only succeeded in polarising much of the population, and causing many civilians to support the I.R.A.

My Grandfather never approved of the I.R.A although his older brother Charlie was a supporter. Instead like many young Irishmen from poor rural areas, John left the country in pursuit of work. Grandfather left Ireland at the age of seventeen and worked as a labourer digging drainage systems on farms all over Scotland. The work was back breaking and tedious. For Granddad and the other young Irishmen there was little choice of employment, and they did the work that many local people did not wish to do.

His work eventually brought him to the small town of Helensburgh where he worked on drainage projects in the town's Hermitage Park. It was then that he met Mary Sharkey whose family came from the same area of Donegal. My Grandmother Mary had an Aunt who ran a boarding house. My Grandfather John and some of his workmates lodged in the house. Mary often visited her Aunt Sally to help out at meal times. After dinner she would often chat to the Irishmen as they played cards in the evening after their long days work. They were a cheerful bunch of men with a strong sense of humour, and the young Mary enjoyed the company.

One Friday evening John was in a particularly good mood. He had worked overtime during the week and his pay packet was heavier than usual. He looked down at Mary's well worn shoes and said to the rest of the company "Do you know what I'm going to tomorrow? I'm going to take Mary to town and buy her a new pair of shoes!" John was true to his word and the next day new the shoes were bought for the young Mary. The couple then began walking out together, and in time became man and wife.

At the outbreak of the First World War my Grandfather like many other Irishmen, joined the British navy to fight for Britain. However when the rebellion erupted in Dublin in 1916 and the British Navy began shelling the Irish capital city, this was a bridge too far for Grandfather and many of his country men who abandoned their posts, and returned home to Ireland. As the penalty for desertion was death Grandfather then travelled back to Scotland to fetch my Grandmother and her two daughters Annie and Gracie to his home village of Mullaghduff in Donegal. It was during this period in my Grandparent's lives that my Uncle Neilly was born. However Britain needed all the manpower it could muster to meet the demands of the Great War they were embroiled in. An amnesty was declared for every Irishman who returned to their ranks. Grandfather gave himself up and joined the Enniskillen Fusiliers. Now in the Army he was sent overseas to continue the fight.

The end in sight

While Neilly lay in that twilight state hovering between life and death, the other struggling souls continued the battle for life. On the 18th of August 1945 the men in Neillys' camp awoke and made their usual trip to the latrines. The air was still and strangely silent. The men felt uneasy and confused. There were no guards in sight. Could this be a trap? Were the guards waiting in hiding for an excuse to fire on them? Then someone noticed the hated Japanese flag, which was normally hoisted up the flag pole at dawn, was missing. Slowly realisation dawned and someone shouted " The bastards have gone"

Soon some local natives appeared, and with gestures and signs, told the men that the Japanese had left in the night. They were later to learn that the war had ended three days before on August the 15th. The reaction to this knowledge was dramatic. Some men sank to their knees and thanked God in prayer. Some stayed standing tears rolling down their ravished faces. Others ran around shouting and screaming, in uncontrolled elation, at the news they never thought they would live to hear. The Thai people at great risk to themselves had rendered great services to the POW and the surviving prisoners would never forget their kindness.

Eventually calm was restored and the men discussed their new liberated situation. They then searched the Japanese quarters for food water, and any medicines or medical items which could be used to help the sick and weak POW. Neilly was sick very very sick and racked with pain. Both lungs were heavily congested. His temperature was soaring. This pneumonia was threatening to take his life. He heard the jubilations of his comrades, yet in his delirious state was unable to rejoice with them.

Later that day after being given doses of quinine and aspirin, Neilly had a vague memory of being carried to a still serviceable locomotive, and beginning the slow and painful journey south. After a short distance, a cry from the leading carriage signalled help. A rescue team was slowly steaming up the track towards them Red Cross flags streaming from either sides of the train. Friends and help at last. Neilly can not remember being given so many pills and injections in one day. He was taken to a field hospital in Kanchanaburi with the other severely sick and emaciated men. There the men received proper medical attention and time to recover from their ordeals. There the men were separated into groups by nationality. Neilly although not happy with this arrangement, understood that this would aid the authorities identify and return POWs to their countries and families.

The home coming

Back in Neillys' small home town of Helensburgh people were celebrating the end of the war. A huge welcome home party was organised for the returning POW survivors. On the day of their homecoming, the sun shone brightly on the cheerful town, decorated with banners and colourful streamers. A handful of men arrived by train and were greeted by all the local dignitaries, and of course joyful families and friends elated and grateful to be reunited with their young men. Street parties exploded throughout the town and lasted for days.

For Neilly's parents it was a confusing and emotional time. The war was over, and happily some of their friend's sons had returned alive. Yet their only son had not. It was six weeks before my grandparents eventually received the wonderful news, their only son Neilly had also survived and it would be another six months before they were to set eyes on their son again.

When the news finally came that Neilly was at last on his way home, my Grandfather, Mother, and her Sister Sadie's husband Paddy, set off to meet him.

They had to travel by bus to the city of Glasgow, where Neilly would be arriving at central station. As the bus drew up at the bus stop on Clyde Street in Helens burgh, my Mother Patsy could see that it was already full. Grandfather spoke to the driver of the bus explaining that they were on their way to meet his son a prisoner of war who was at last coming home. "We don't mind standing, if you will just please let us on." he pleaded. The bus driver shook his head, and said he was most sorry but could not allow three passengers to travel without seats, all the way to the city. Hearing my Grandfather's story some kind hearted passengers on the bus, were happy to give up their seats and allow the little group to travel in their place. My Grandfather was moved by this spontaneous act of kindness, and on the hours journey to the city, frequently shed a small tear.

After this gap in time, a train steamed slowly into Glasgow central station. A number of passengers alighted. Lastly, a small frail thin figure descended on to the platform. He heaved his heavy kit bag on to his narrow shoulders, and walked slowly and carefully through the hissing clouds, pulsing from the steam train. Three lonely figures hearts aching, watched him emerge from the hot mist. My Mother stifled a scream and ran towards him. My grandfather strode quickly towards him followed by Paddy. My mother only seventeen suddenly stopped running and stood still in shock. She had been expecting to see the big brother she fondly remembered. Instead she was looking at a little wizened old man, she did not recognise. My uncle Neilly was just twenty seven years of age.

After the reunion the four made their way to the northern line station, and boarded a train at Queen Street which would carry them back to their small seaside home town. Arriving at Helensburgh the little group walked the short distance back to my grandparent's tenement flat in Grant Street. Their journey being interrupted by a few friends and neighbours out shopping, who suddenly realised that Neilly had indeed at last come home. A few steps forward then pauses, tears and hugs, from well wishers, and then the last push for home. As the tired little group were crossing the old railway bridge, which led into Grant Street, Patsy's young heart skipped a beat. Looking down from the bridge into the street below, she could see an assortment of welcome home banners flapping in the breeze, and crowds of smiling singing people.

Descending the steps of the railway bridge Patsy now was able to recognise the song they were singing. It was a song popular at the time, written by Cole Porter." *Don't Fence Me in."* The song was new to Neilly at the same time it was also very familiar.

Oh give me land, lots of land, under starry skies above,
Don't fence me in
Let me ride through the wide open country that I love
Don't fence me in

Let me be by myself in the evening breeze
Listen to the murmur of the cotton wood trees
Send me off forever, but I ask you please
Don't fence me in

Let my straddle my old saddle underneath the western skies
Let me wander over yonder till I see the mountains rise
I want to ride to the ridge where the west commences
Gaze at the moon till I loose my senses
I can't look at hobbies and I can't stand fences
Don't fence me in
Don't fence me in

As Neilly and the others descended the last steps of the bridge over the railway line and walked towards their happy neighbours, the small crowd cheered and clapped the brave soldier who had survived the war. My Grandfather steered his son through the crowds, politely thanking the folk for the welcome. Neilly's Father then guided him to the close entrance of their flat

The struggle to climb the three flights of stairs to his parent's home was so very difficult. It was like the last lap of a very long race. His father shouldered his kit bag while Paddy and his youngest sister Patsy supported him throughout the climb. Once inside Neilly sank down on his knees and sobbed. His Mother did not speak but knelt beside her son and held him tightly in her arms. As the burning tears flowed from his worn out eyes, and his thin frame shook and trembled, Neilly knew that he really had survived the horrors of that death railway. Yet he also knew that these horrors would return, and waking or sleeping, he would remember them always. Neilly knew that at present even on the softest warmest day, he would be unable to close his eyes, and be caressed by any soothing sun, for the razor sharp winds of memory, could return to slash and shatter the pleasure of every moment.

Memories and illness return

The days and weeks after Neillys' return were slow and quiet. He was still physically weak, and suffered recurrent bouts of Malaria. During one particularly severe episode representatives from the army arrived at the house, and wished to take Neilly to a military hospital for treatment. My Mother clearly remembers my Grandfather refusing to allow Neilly to go. "He has been away for six years, and if you take him now, he will never come back." Neilly was cared for at home by local GP Dr. Harold Scott, and nursed by his parents and sisters, who took turns all day and through the night, sitting by his bedside, trying to cool his raging fever and chase away his nightmarish hallucinations. When his condition improved Neilly wrote a poignant tribute to Duncan, in the form of a poem written on the back of a letter of thanks received from King George at Buckingham Palace.

Neilly and Owenie meet again

Eventually Neilly recovered enough to journey to the city of Glasgow. News had reached him that a reunion meeting of POWs was to take place, and although still weak from his recent illness he was anxious to meet his friend Owenie Burke who had also survived the camps. The meeting place was only a short walk from the train station. As he entered the hall his name and regiment were announced to the group. Neilly looked slowly around the assembled group of men.

The aftermath of death railway affected POW differently. Although some showed only minor problems many others had severe physical and mental problems. A few were unable to cope with returning to normal life and committed suicide. There were a few listless and lost looking souls in the group gathered before him. Others were nervous and agitated. Yet some although still frail, had the light of hope in their eyes, and were attempting jokes with their companions.

Within minutes Neilly was surrounded by fellow POWs. Some faces he recognised and others not. For a brief moment he thought he saw his childhood friend Duncan among the faces. His heart was heavy, for he knew Duncan would never leave that terrible camp, never return to family and friends. Suddenly close to him a face he did know and loved, his brave hearted comrade Owenie Burke. Both men were elated to find one another again.

The rest of the reunion was spent enjoying refreshments of tea and sandwiches, catching up with news, and revelling in the pleasure of seeing old friends once more. Time passed quickly in that emotional yet happy atmosphere, and soon it was time, for the moment at least, to say goodbye to old friends. Owenie invited Neilly back to his home. He wanted Neilly to meet his Father and Sister Rita. By now Neilly was completely worn out and exhausted, yet did not wish to reject his friends offer of hospitality.

Meeting Rita

When the two men arrived at Owenie's family home only Owenie's sister was there to welcome them, and welcome them she did, with warmth, kindness, and good humour. Rita was a young woman with a warm and loving personality coupled with wisdom far beyond her years. She immediately felt sympathy for her brother's companion. Rita had spent months patiently supporting Owenie back into his new life at home. She also knew that Neilly had also suffered, perhaps even more than her brother, and even now was still suffering, a past he could not at present escape. She settled Neilly down at the kitchen table in front of the open fire. Then started preparing a meal of soup bread and cheese, all the while chattering brightly to try and lift his spirits.

Neilly tried hard to be sociable but was feeling more and more unwell. He was becoming unbearably hot. His head hurt abominably, and sweat soaked through his clothing. He tried to focus on Rita standing by the cooker, now with a concerned expression on her young face. Yet it was not Rita's concerned face he saw, it was Duncan's. Neilly cried out and tried to move towards him. His legs would not hold him, and he collapsed on to the kitchen floor where he lay shaking uncontrollably. His last sensation was the feeling of Rita's strong young arms around him before he lost consciousness.

On his collapse Owenie had gone quickly to fetch a doctor who diagnosed double pneumonia and recommended immediate hospitalisation. As these were the days before the introduction of the National Health Service, this was out of the question. Instead he was cared for in Owenie's home and nursed by Rita until arrangements were made for his return home to Helensburgh. Back home Neilly was again cared for by the local family doctor and nursed by his parents and sisters who took turns sitting by his bed trying to cool his fever. During his weeks of recovery Rita and Owenie visited often and a strong bond grew between the two young people. In the young Rita, sympathy and growing friendship slowly became stronger emotions, of love and devotion. In the young man to gratitude and friendship was added love loyalty, and passion for the lovely Rita. Both knew that they would continue to see one another, and that indeed was what happened.

Patsy and Ross and the weddings

Once back home Neilly was to find tension and frustration in the family. His youngest sister Patsy now eighteen was determined to marry her boyfriend of two years. Ross Neil was just nineteen and was still an apprentice tradesman. Both Neillys' parents were at the end of their tether. My mother Patsy always strong willed and with a fiery temper, was making life difficult for everyone. Their four older daughters had all recently married, and the family were not in the position to fund another wedding. They also felt that mum and dad were too young to take this very big step, coupled with this; my Fathers' wages were too little to support a wife and home. However Patsy soon won the support of her only brother, who realised that his youngest sister would not be swayed from her chosen path. With his usual generosity of spirit Neilly offered to pay for the young people's wedding with his POW compensation. The princely sum of thirty pounds paid by the government to all 2nd world war soldiers who had been imprisoned during the war.

Over the next few months Neilly and Rita saw a great deal of one another, and although deeply in love, had to be patient, and wait a little longer to be married. For the sake of peace and family harmony my Mother and Father's wedding took priority. They were married on December the 28th, 1945 in the church of St Joseph in their home town of Helens burgh and with

Neillys' financial help even managed a short honeymoon in nearby Rothesay. Soon after, in an effort to increase their income Mum and Dad moved south to Yorkshire where they both worked for a number of years.

When Neilly and Rita did marry their honeymoon was spent in my parents' very modest rented accommodation in Middlesbrough. When Mother became pregnant with me, she and my Father returned home to Helensburgh.

The early years

Neilly and Rita also settled in Helensburgh. Their first home was a tiny upstairs flat in the lovely Colquhoun Square in the centre of town. My parents rented accommodation was only a few streets away. As a small child I was able to visit often, and have fun playing with their first born Johnnie. However our home was more spartan, and had less basic amenities than my cousin's. A forgotten crumbling but and ben cottage, which once would have been surrounded by rolling green fields, and babbling brooks, now found itself in the middle of a working wood yard, hemmed in and overlooked by more modern high flats outside the yard. Our property had an outside toilet. Although common in old properties, it was more difficult than usual to use, as the whole wood yard workforce had adopted it as their own. This infuriated my young Mother, who had to clean the facility.

One day when she had spotted a worker going into "our toilet" she gave me the key with the instruction to run to the end of the garden, and lock the offender in. My mother was not one to argue with especially when she was angry. Although only four I tripped out in my little blue slippers, stood on log, placed the key in the door, and turned the lock. Then ran as fast as I could, back to my mother in the cottage "Did he say anything my mother asked? " Well" I replied "he didn't say anything but he shouted, you Fucking Bastard". The conclusion of the incident was a smashed door, as the man escaped back to his work mates. As my Father was working late that night Neilly was summoned to replace the toilet door. Over the years Neilly was always on hand for both family and friends, whenever there was a need.

Always on hand

When I was still quite a small child I became ill and suffered severe abdominal pain. My Mother called the doctor who suspected appendicitis, and quickly called for an ambulance. Mother sent my little brother Terence, who was just two years old on his own to run to Neilly and Rita's home where he could be looked after, while she went with me in the ambulance. As the vehicle was driving along the road Neilly ran out and frantically waved the ambulance to a halt. When the driver opened the doors Neilly jumped in, his boots still covered in hard cement. When Terence arrived at his house Neilly had just come in from his work brick laying on a nearby building site. He travelled with my Mother and me to the Western Hospital in Glasgow. I spent a truly horrible week alone in that hospital. I suppose I was somewhat demanding of the nursing staff. I had long hair which became tangled when I was sleeping. In the morning I would ask them to comb and plait my hair. I was ignored, and would then begin to shout and yell at the nurse who mainly worked in my ward. One day for spite she came over to my bed and picked up the only toy I had with me, a soft little black and white toy dog. "There's a child in another ward needs this more than you" She spat the words out, and quickly disappeared with my dog. For the rest of my stay I shrieked and screamed every time I saw the woman, demanding that she brought back my toy dog. She never did.

Eventually I was allowed to get dressed. They had found no serious illness and although I would often still vomit after eating, once all over the nurse I disliked, I could now go home. Out in the corridor I was overjoyed to see Neilly my Grandmother and my Mother all waiting to take me home. Back home I still cried at night in bed for my little toy dog .Once back home my Father bought me a beautiful walking doll with auburn hair the same colour as my Mother's. However although the doll was very nice, I still cried in the night for my favourite toy dog.
Some weeks later, my big cousin Frank Smith arrived at our home. He was wearing a tartan jerkin which he unzipped. As he did so the head of tiny black and brown puppy popped out.

I was ecstatic the puppy was for me. Now I had a real dog. I called him Scottie though he bore no resemblance to the traditional Scottish terrier.

From children to teenagers

Time went on, and all the children of the Families, began to become teenagers, and what a wild bunch we were. There was about twenty of us. Our ages ranged from early to late teens. To accommodate their expanding family Neilly and Rita had moved to a larger house in Stucklekie Road on the outskirts of the town. Oh what wonderful times we all had in that happy house. At New Year the house bursting at the seams with Hogmanay revellers. I remember one year the living room was so crowded that two of the boys unscrewed the door into the room to allow more space for the party goers. There was music and laughter all night long. Those who could sing sang their hearts out, and those who could not, sang with them. I still remember my cousin Owen, easily the most handsome of the McGinley boys using a sweeping brush as a microphone, and belting out his version of Rod Stewart's Maggie May. Then Hugo on the banjo, and Raymond on guitar performing the theme from the film Deliverance, "Duelling Banjo". Then there was my future husband Ian knocking out a tune on the old untuned piano, and everyone singing along to Obla dee Obla da life goes on etc.

NEILLY'S SON NEIL'S, PARTY RECOLLECTIONS

'THE BELLS AT NUMBER 37

The brothers were sitting on New Years Day on the Sittooterie at Mullaghduff in Helensburgh, looking over the Clyde to the Tower in the Home Farm at Rosneath. 'Some view! Eh?'Aye! You get an unrestricted view of the Peninsula even wae they trees there!

'New Year's morning, and not a sore heid between us!'
'Remember the parties we used to have at 37?'
'I never missed one! I remember them all'
The brother, shook his head' the laugh lines in his face creasing, ' you'll be lucky to remember any N'erdays at 37, the states you used to get into!'

The Parties at 37 Stuckleckie Road were legend.

The Christmas decorations which had survived the previous week would still be up. A real Christmas tree covered with silver tinsel, fairy lights and shiny bobbles with a wee petticoated fairy on top. The tree would be planted in the ash'es bucket, filled with soil from the garden and covered with Christmas paper. The tree was sometimes a wee bit squeegee. Some years a silver star would top the tree which would sit in the alcove at the window. The Star in the Bright Sky.

Christmas cards were suspended on a string above the fifestone fireplace the Faither had built. Logs would be burning on the fire. The guard would be up. The wee Hummels would be on the mantlepiece. On the side board would be a little straw roofed crib, with the head of the St Joseph statuette stuck on with the forerunner to Superglue. The three wise men would be in the Crib now. Some holy Christmas cards from the Aunties and from Ireland would be placed round the crib.

'A real Christmas tree is nice but you can still be hoovering those pine needles up in February'

Beside the Nativity scene sat the wee red Fidelity record player the 'Big Ones' got for Christmas many years earlier. A pile of records would sit alongside the record player. Silver tinsel framed the oval mirror and the brass plate on the wall. The wee cuckoo clock which hung on the wall had given up cuckooing years previously. The framed picture of the Sacred Heart would also get the silver tinsel treatment! A sprig of berried holly from the Chapel house would be pinned above the brass plate and above the Sacred Heart. There would also be a sprig of holly above the crucifix the brother won for being dux. The holly berries would be starting to get a wee bit shriveled up after over a week on the wall. The brass candlesticks, on top of the mantle piece and the other brasses would be polished with Brasso by the brother who was good at polishing. Seats, including the red stools from the kitchen, would be set round the living room and there was room for four or five on the couch. A couple could sit on the arms of the couch.

The Twins would organize the purvey.
'Nuts and crisps and things'
'Sausage Rolls. Aye the wee wans'
'Aye, that sort of thing'
Assorted nuts and crisps would be spread around the room on saucers.
'Stop eating them. They are for after!'
Plates with shortbread and sultana cakes. Plates of wee sausage rolls . Plates of wee sausages on wee wooden sticks. Plates of pickled onions and lumps of cheese on wee wooden sticks. Plates of cheese and pineapple cubes on wee wooden sticks.
'Fancy!'
Wee savoury biscuits with a squirt of spreaded, cheese and a pickled onion or a prawn on top.
'Fancy!'
Wee cheesy biscuits.
'Keep your hands off!'
Plates filled with triangular sandwiches with the crusts cut off.
'Very Posh!'
Grub for everyone.
The food would be covered with a table cloth but any attempts to stop the food being sampled were futile.
'There will be nothing left for the Bells. You are a crowd of gannets!'
Glasses would be borrowed from the Royal Bar and laid out on the kitchen table. The brothers ordered two eleven gallon barrels; one of lager and one of heavy.
'Are you sure two barrels will be enough?
'Aye! Plenty.'
There were cans of lager and export in reserve.

There would be no Invitation List. No one was invited to our parties. Everyone just arrived.

All friends and family and all kinds of waifs and strays would end up at our parties. It was an open door affair, literally.

One year the pal wouldn't let his future wife join in the festivities and as she knocked the door was heard singing the then popular song 'I hear you knockin' but you can't come in!'

'Don't be drinking too much before the bells' admonished Mammy when the brothers were leaving to pick up the carry out and glasses from the pub where the brother worked during the holidays. The gaffer called the brother 'The Bull', a reference to his supposed prowess with the ladies.

'Aye the burds were queuing up for him outside the pub at shutting time,' Jimmy (Hugo's maw called him 'Nelly') Graham used to say.

'Aye the Bull used to sneak out the back door and up the back pen to get away from the women! Aye the Bull was some man!' I always wondered why he wanted to get away from them! I'll have to ask the brother. The brother would deny the allegations but I think he had previous convictions.

The barrels were set up in the kitchen with foot pumps. A few trial pints would be sampled by the brothers to ensure that the quality of the ale was up to scratch for the guests. Not guests but you know what I mean.

'Aye it's as clear as a bell'

Beer on tap was very popular. Everyone enjoyed a pint more when the pubs were shut, especially the underage brother and his pals who spent the night in the kitchen 'in charge of the pumps'.

The brother's pal, Broon , never said a word from one year to the other but at New Year you couldn't shut him up.

'A great party! A great party!" Broon would repeat all night.

Bottles of Bacardi or Bromista, which was a cheaper version, Gin, Vodka and whisky, littered the kitchen table. Cans of beer were stacked underneath it. Help your self department. Everyone put their bottles on the table and helped themselves.

The night would start quietly. Waiting on the bells.
'A wee plate of soup, to put a lining on your stomach.'
'Aye! That's a good idea. A wee plate of soup will go down a treat.'
'It won't be long now.'
The last hour of the year always seemed to drag in.
'All things considered, last year wisnae so bad!'
'Naw it was not.'
Idle chit chat.
The last fifteen minutes would be in slow motion.
The Town Clock would ring in the New Year. We would all go out the back door and would listen for the ships on the Clyde sounding their horns wishing everyone on the sea and at shore a Happy New Year.
'Can you hear the ships?
'Aye, remember the racket they used to make when the Clyde was busy, in the old days'

Back into the house, Mum and Dad and the nine of us would all hold hands in a big circle and sing 'Auld Lang Syne'

'Happy New Year!' 'Happy New Year!' We would all shake hands and exchange kisses.

'Happy New Year!' We weren't a kissy kind of family and this was probably the only time in the year we showed much affection. 'Happy New Year!'

The wee red Fidelity record player would hammer out the usual songs to warm the night up. 'Put on 'Ah belong to Glasgow' by Will Fyfe' suggested Mammy.

'Followed by Bridie Gallagher singing 'the Homes of Donegal' interjected the Faither.

'Never mind, Bridie Gallagher give us Rory Gallagher' piped up the brother.

The wee red fidelity record player had the capacity to play six records in succession but the turntable would slow down after the fifth song. The wee red Fidelity record player would play and we'd all join in.

'I'm only a common old working chap as anyone here can see'.

The lager and beer would continue to be tested.

'I've just stepped in to see you all, I'll only stay awhile, I long to see how your gettin' on. I long to see your smile''. The Faither's request would be playing.

Things would be warming up nicely.

Mrs Cranston from next door would come in after the bells. Her husband Bob would never make the bells. We would get a visit from Bob in the morning. A half bottle of Port and a wee miniature of Drambuie would have been included in the New Year carryout.

Mrs. Cranston would imbibe only at New Year and this was her tipple.

Mammy was a bit superstitious and believed that a dark haired first foot would bring luck. Sometimes Mammy would send one of us out the back door to come in the front door, lump of coal in hand with the black mongrel Gyp. Wee Jock was always a welcome first foot. 'Joe Sweeney'a Karl Denver skiffle song he had learned from the wee red fidelity record player would get big licks. The wee red Fidelity record player would be switched off.

Visitors would start arriving soon after the Bells.
The front door knocker would go. Gyp the first foot would bark.

'Happy New Year!' Happy New Year!'
The front door knocker would go again. Gyp would bark again.

'Happy New Year!' 'Happy New Year!'
The door would eventually be left open. An open invitation. Literally.

'Happy New Year!' Happy New Year!'
Gyp would get fed up barking and would retire upstairs away from the turmoil.

The brother's pal who didn't like getting called 'Peem' would be an early arrival.

'Happy New Year Neilly. Happy New Year Rita'.
The brother's pal would call the parents by their first names. All the other pals except the lodger called them Mr. and Mrs. McGinley. Peem would sing a song about

coloured guys sitting at the back of buses in Alabama he had learned from a Pete Seeger LP.
'We Shall Overcome!'

'Deep in my heart I do believe!'
'Goneyerselpeem!'
'Dontcallmepeem!'
'Sorry Peem!'
'Give us a wee tune Hugo' the Faither would sort of request.
'A wee minute Neilly, I'm jist tuning the banjo' was the standard reply from the lodger.
'Come on. A wee tune Hugo!' a few minutes later.
Hugo knew the Faither got irritated with the tuning, and that nobody in the house would notice if it was out of key. He would always take Faither to the edge with the tuning lark.
'I've just to get the F string right Neilly!' riled Hugo.
I think the lodger knew what the Faither was thinking about the F string!
A wee bluegrass solo from Hugo would get the house jumping.
The Faither would sit in his chair, a wee bottle of Guinness at his feet and a half of the cratur in his hand and that would be his position for the duration. Mammy would sit on the floor in front of the Faithers seat.
'Would you like a wee hauf' the visitors would offer a drink from their N'erday bottle.
'Naw we're fine.'
'Naw ah'm fine the noo John. Ah'll maybe get a wee one later.'
'Auch come on Mr McGinley! It's New Year!'

Awe right. Jist a wee one then' The Faither didnae stand a chance at Ne'rday.
  'Would you like a wee bit of shortbread?'
"Or maybe, a wee sausage roll?"
'Do you think there will be enough to go round?'
'Wae the weather out there I don't think many wise souls will be out tonight.'
  We weren't expecting too many wise souls.
'Come on. A wee tune Hugo!'
'I'm jist about there Neilly' the lodger would say slipping the banjo over his shoulder.

The cousins would arrive in taxis.
The Cousin Liz's man could play the guitar. We had a piano in the living room, which the Faither hoped one of us would manage to master. None of us ever did. Nobody could play a note. Someone would usually give the keys a rattle at New Year.
The cousin's man didn't bother with the tuning and quickly launched into his repertoire of popular songs.
'OobladeeOobladda' would get a battering. Everyone, hands raised, endangering the last of the Christmas decorations on the ceiling, would join in.
'Oobladee! Obladda ! Life Goes On! Ohhh! Ohhh! Ohhh! Life Goes On!'
'Eleanor Rigby.'
'Help'
'The Times They Are a Changin'
 Everyone joined in whether they knew the words or not.
  'What about a song from Faither?'
'Aye a song from Uncle Neilly!'

Gie us 'Moonlight o'er Malaya', a song the Faither had learned as a POW.
'Sshhhh it's too early.'
'What about 'The Thin Red Line'? An old Argyll's song.
'Cheer up m'lads! Cheer up m'lads! You'll maybe get your chance'
'What about 'Hail! Hail!'
'Oh Naw!
'Aye Goneyersellfaither!
The Faither widnae need much encouragement.
Hugo would plonk out the first few keys.

'Hail!'
The Faither would shut his eyes when he was singing.
 'Old Scotch Mother Mine' would get an annual airing and sometimes a wee tear would sneak through the Faither's closed eyes.
'Naw, not 'the Old Bog Road'. "You know I don't like that song,"

"The boys will give us a song".
The brother would sing 'The Juice of the Barley' solo while we worked out what songs we'd sing. We always sang the same songs; it was just the order that was sometimes different. The brother was good at 'Juice of the Barley.'

 The brothers would go through a repertoire of Clancy Brothers and Dubliners songs which had been well played on the wee red fidelity record player. 'The Holy Ground, The Irish Rover, Brennan on the Moor, The Leaving of Liverpool, Were off to Dublin in the Green, and The One Road' were some of the songs they would

sing. 'The Old Triangle' would sometimes get jingle jangled. Mammy liked the brothers singing.
'What's the Life of a Man?' a Macalmans song was also a favourite. The joiner and the brother would sing that.
'What's the Life of a Man any more than a leaf? A man has his season so why should he grieve?' Cheery!
The red haired cousin, Terence would sing 'The Wild Colonial Boy.'
 'He was born and bred in Ire-land in a place called Castle Maine'
'Whisky in the Jar' would be next by the red haired cousin's red haired brother Tommy.

'I met with Captain Farrow and his money he was countin''
The Faither had the red hair, but none of the brothers or sisters had inherited it. I think some of the brothers would have liked the red hair.
The other cousin's man wisnae a singer, but he would do a dance that was a cross between the Twist, the Shake and Jive. He was some mover!
The lodger's brother would sing 'Black Velvet Band'. The lodger would slag him.

 The brother's theme tune was the 'Joe Dempsey' song and knee clapping routine. A sort of Country and Western, Dashing White Sergeant, YeeeeHahhhh! Instead of Hooooch!
'Joe Dempsey's been and gone...Left last night with his oilskins on!'

The brother would sometimes 'Pea on the Green fields of Dundee' and 'Let his hair hang low' which was as risqué as it would get.
'Sally for a song!'
'I'll sing along with Carol.'
The cousins would sing 'The Boys from the County Armagh'.
'Best of order now!'
'It's my old Irish home…..Far across the foam'.
Mammy liked that song as she had Murphy relations from Newry and Crossmaglen.
'That's the barrel of Heavy finished!'
'I told you we should have ordered two!'
'There's plenty cans.'
'Aye!'
The brother would sing 'Summertime' the veins in his neck busting, but could reach the high notes alright!

'Fish are jumpin' and the cotton is high!'
A quick gargle at his pint to ease the larynx and maybe he'd sing 'You'll Never Walk Alone'. We'd all join in, hands raised above our heads like in the Jungle.

The brother's pals, the joiner and the spark, were currant buns but they would join in too. Maybe wae their hands no just as high as ours! The decorations on the ceiling were safe with them. Sandy and Gillie were all right. We would go together on the train to Old Firm games and meet after the game when there would be a wee bit of banter and kidology depending upon which side won and who was celebrating.

Sandy and the brother would do a morbid duet 'What's the life of a Man' that would have everybody greeting.

'A leaf has its season so why should we grieve?
Although through this life we appear fine and gay.
Like a leaf we must wither and soon fade away.'
Just the sort of song to get the party goin!

'Fauderee! Faulderra!'

The cousins and the brothers and the sisters would join in with Mammy singing *'Fauderee! Faulderra*! *With a Nap-sack on my Back'.* Remember the times we had across the Fruin, Uncle Neilly?' We would recall childhood picnics spent across Glen Fruin.

'Gie us they Tubular Bells you are always on aboot' The other brother would always sing a song called 'Patrick'. He was into Mick Oakfield's Tubular Bells which didn't have any words so he couldn't sing Tubular Bells! He always just sang 'Patrick'

'Partrick, my painter, painter of art!'
He was a mechanic! He would sing it down his nose the way Gerry Rafferty did.

The other brother used to try and sing 'You'll Never Walk Alone' before the other brother sang it. If it had already been sung, he'd sing 'The Lonely Bana Strand' with his eyes shut like the Faithers, having practiced the words at the cracked mirror in the toilet. The brother wondered if the other brother shut his eyes when he was practicing the singing. 'If he did he widnae see himself in the mirror!' he concluded.

The brother from up the dreel came back doon the dreel with a selection of Johnnies gone to Melville Castles and Braes at Killiecrankies and Balls at Kirriemuirs and Bunnets from Bonnie Dundee. He got some slaggin from the brothers for his cultural divergence and would redeem himself by singing 'James Connolly'.
'No party songs now.'
'James Connolly' is a Socialist song'
The brother learned a song about working on the railway which had about twenty five verses and he knew them all and insisted on singing every single one of them.
'In Eighteen hundred and forty five when Daniel O'Connell he was alive, when Daniel O'Connell he was alive and working on the railway'
'Daniel is a poof!'
'Naw! O'Connell! Daniel O'Connell I'm singing about.'
'I was wearing corduroy britches; diggin ditches; dodgin' hitches' is indelibly printed in my memory. There have been nights I have not slept a wink with the words 'In Eighteen hundred and Forty something' going through my head. Weeks after the party! There should have been a health warning given before the brother put on the corduroy troosers!
'The Twins will give us a song.'
'Aye come on girls'
'Ah don't sing'
You can so!' persuaded Mammy. 'You can sing together.'
'You've not given us a song yet Mammy. You sing first then we'll sing' suggested the other sister.

'Give us 'Old Maid in a Garret'.
'I hate that song' Mammy would say but would sing it brilliantly nevertheless.

'Ah can cook and ah can sew ah can keep a hoose right tidy'
　If she was in form, and she usually was, Mammy would also give us her Salome song and dance routine which was always the highlight of the night.
'O! Salome! Salome!' singing, Mammy would wiggle and wriggle and glide round the room in Eastern pose.
　'O! Salome! Salome!'
'Dancing there with her feet all bare'
　Brilliant. More! More!
'Gone Yersel Mrs McGinley.
'Goneyersel Auntie Rita'
'Did you ever see the photo of my Maw in a grass skirt?'
　'Four Green Fields' followed by the 'Galway Shawl' from the Twins would get rapturous approval.
'then strangers came and tried to take them from me'

'The Four green fields are the four Provinces you know'
'They are rerr singers'
'Aye! So they are. They are some turns the two o' them'
'Do you know any Daniel songs?'
'Wait till I think'
'Daniel's a poof'
'No he is not'
'Ah don't care what he is he cannae half sing and he has put the Rosses on the map.'
'The Rosses was on the map long before Daniel'
'He's too squeaky clean for my liking!'

'What about that wan 'My Donegal Shore? You know that wan. Aye sing that.'
'I'm not sure of the words but I'll try it.'
The sister would sing it word perfectly, Donegal brogue as well!
'That's the barrel of lager finished as well!'
'I told you we should have got two!
'I think maybe we overdone the testing!'
'You have all had plenty!'
'Another barrel wouldn't have gone amiss. The pubs are shut tomorrow.'
'No matter how much you got it would never be enough!'

'Whosnextfrasong?'
At first no one would want to sing but after a few bevvies they'd be queuing up. They would be practicing in the toilet, raring to go.
There was sometimes the odd lovers tiff or wee skirmish but generally the parties were all sweetness and light. The sisters would sometimes sing a song about an old woman who lived in the woods and who stuck a pen knife in her baby's back down by some river! Mammy would tell them not to sing it but they would just carry on.

Henry, the Faither's cousin would sometimes wander in. A bottle of whiskey in his hand, and a few bottles of his home brew in his pockets. Henry's home brew was legend. It was dynamite. Henry would annually declare his undying love for my Mother. "Ah love you Rita you are a great woman! "You're a lucky lucky man Neilly!" "Aye Ah know that Henry!" Henry would usually give

us a long song and fall asleep on the chair. Some man the Henry!
Scoodie, no matter what condition he was in always turned up and sang his Tommy Makem numbers to perfection with his eyes shut as well. Sometimes he wasn't fit to speak but wouldn't miss a verse out of his songs.

Hugo would eventually get tuned up and warmed up and show us the time he spent upstairs practicing on the banjo hadn't gone to waste. He had constructed the Gibson himself and could make the banjo talk. He was equally good on the guitar. Self taught. 'Do Do Do Do Do Do Do Do Do' 'Deliverance' 'Dual on Banjos'. The place would be jumping. It would be going Bell Ting!
'I'll give you a wee James Taylor number. 'Carolina'
'I'm off to Carolina in my mind.'
The Faither would be happy the tuning was over.
'Gonyersel Hugo!'
'Give us 'Carrick Fergus!'
Hugo introduced us to the beautiful melodic song 'Carrick Fergus' which was a great favourite of the brothers until they visited the place when they missed the boat on the way back from Peggy's funeral. The brothers stopped in a few places that day. Funerals can be thirsty old work all right!

'I wish I was in Carrick Fergus'
We should have known better. All the regalia, was up in the streets. We ventured into a 'Social Club', the only licensed premises open in Carrick Fergus on a Sunday. The brothers were thirsty. When we walked into the long bar, not unlike the old Mermaid Bar, everything

went quiet and everyone turned round and looked at the four brothers.

We were in the wrong place. There were no beautiful maidens in this Carrick Fergus. 'See the shoulders on them! Good Ulster farming stock.'

'Shhhh!

'Beef to their heels like Mullingar heifers!'

Shhhh!

The men were big as well!

The brother was paranoid that we'd be recognised by our names or by what we drank. They could tell by what you drank.

'Don't ask for Smithwicks or Harp Lager whatever you do.' admonished the brother.

The brother who was on the Coke said he'd just get his own.

'They'll ask you if you want Coca Cola or Pepsi! I hope you know the right answer.' spluttered the paranoid brother.

'A bottle of Boyne Mineral Water instead of Ballygowan Water. That'll do me!'

'Ah hope you choke on it'

'Don't call me Mick' raved the terrified brother when he spotted a big ,wide- foreheaded, mustachioed, bull necked Ulsterman carrying a tray of drinks and heading towards the table we had selected in the corner. 'I hope that Guinness is not for me!'

The brother who was on the Boyne Water introduced William James to the brothers. 'William James was at the Cup Final, I was telling William James at the bar we couldnae get tickets.'

'Isn't that's right? Had to watch the Teddy Bears getting beat on the telly. It was terrible!'
'That Boyne Water is affecting the brother' thought the other brother, 'He'll be giving it the 'Old Bangers and Mash' next!'
The brother who was on the Boyne Water managed to convince the inquisitive Ulsterman that we regularly attended Ibrox without actually saying that! We drank up swiftly and left the lovely Carrick Fergus with no desire to return. The brothers have never 'wished they were in Carrick Fergus' since.

A Dumbarton influence crept into the proceedings and songs like 'Little Old Wine Drinker Me' or 'Stand by Yer Man' and 'One Day at a Time', anthems of that Parish, would be sung by a daughter of the Rock.
The brother's brother-in-law would play the accordion upside down!
'Would it no be easier playing it the right way up?'

'Have you ever seen Jimmi Hendrix playing the guitar?'
'Whit?'
   'Goneyerselpeem!'
'Peem didn't seem to mind getting called Peem.
Owensie and Mick McIlroy were regular attenders and would give us a number on Hugo's guitar. Neither of them had mastered the instrument but they were tryers and could play it better than any of us the Faither would say.
 Dermot brought his faither Harry round with his fiddle one year. Harry would play a few jigs and reels and would have our feet tapping.
The King would make a cameo appearance.

'Jailhouse Rock.' The King loved an audience and the audience loved the King.

'More! More!'

'Wooden Heart'. The King would sing the German verse with an accent straight from the Tower or the La Scala. Hitler singing Rock 'n Roll!

'O.K. folks!' the King believed the hype. 'Jailhouse Rock' again for an encore.'

'That's all folks. I'm moving on but I never miss the McGinley parties. Nice People.'

Isn't that right Mr and Mrs McGinley?'

'Aye that's right Billy.'

Biddy thought he was Elvis reincarnated. The King was some turn!

The night wouldn't be complete without 'Maggie May'. The brother did a brilliant version of Rod Stewart's song. Dressed in bright red full length leather coat (the Faither said he was like a pillar-box), navy blue and white double platform boots, hair streaked like a chaffinch (the brother's description) substituting a sweeping brush for the microphone stand, the brother would launch into action.

'Wake up Maggie! Ah think ah got got somethin to say to you!'

The place would be jam packed with seats round the wall and bodies strewn on the floor. Every space taken. The brother would still find room to dance about and swing the brush like Rod! 'Watch the decorations!' Head back like Rod, brush above his head, red coat open and swinging, the brother would glide around the room belting it out.

'It's Late September and I really should be back at school.'

'Wan singer! Wan song now!
  'Last time now!
  Wake up Maggie……..'

'Aye! He wakens up Maggie Ah right!'
The King didn't like anyone outdoing him. The brother would always outdo him!

'The brother used to sing this song to different words
He was a devil for the style

And he never had trouble pullin' burds

*In the Imps or in the Bar-L
Our aftershave we'd smell
He'd Wake up Maggie
And half the scheme as well*!'

The singing would go on into the wee small hours. The living room door would come off its hinges with all the through traffic and be hammered back up the next day or the day after. It would sometimes lie in the lobby for longer than that!
There would be a party in the kitchen, spilling into the lobby and onto the staircase with the main event in the living room. People would hear the music and come in. It would be bedlam.
 'Give us Oobladee again!

'Desmond had a barrow in the market square'
'Gone Yersel Ian'
'Wan singer! Wan song now!
   'Naw! NaeWan singer! Wan song! C'mon everybody join in!'
'In Eighteen Hundred and Forty six I changed my trade to carrying bricks.'
'No party songs now!'

'Hail! Hail! The Celts are here!'

'Daniel is a poof!'

'That's enough!'
'If you are going to the game tomorrow you better get some sleep!'

Then there would be more kisses and cuddles as the revellers left.
'Aye a Good New Year. I hope it's a Good one for you.'
'Does anyone fancy the New Year Swim?'
'Aye we can visit the Aunties wae Faither after the Swim!'

'In Eighteen Hundred and…………'
   'Where's Gyp?'

Happy days!

Back in the Sittooterie at Mullaghduff, under the starlit sky, it was getting cold.

'You can see the frost glistening on the single bloom on the wee red rose tree.'

'Aye! It's beautiful. A bargain buy from Woolies.'

'Aye! You can remember bits of the parties at Number 37 right enough' conceded the brother.

'But you could write a book about the bits you missed! I'll fill in the blanks for you sometime!'

'Aye! As the Man said 'some McGinleys can drink and some can't!'

When you look back, Mammy and the Faither surely had big hearts putting up with it all. Eh?

Nellus
1 January 2001

We were all young and eager to for excitement. Thirsting to run with the wind, drink the moon and the stars, and sail on the summit of a wave. At the same time for us life seemed to float forever on the sweet notes of a soft song, and none of us realised that for all of us, there would be some sadness ahead.

Hugo and Billy Niven were also part of Neillys' family. The boys had lost their parents when both were still quite young teenagers. Hugo left home to find work in London. In the meantime Billy and his sister Margaret married and moved on. Eventually Hugo returned to Helensburgh. Now homeless Hugo knocked on the door at number 37 and asked if he could stay the night. Without hesitation Neilly and Rita took Hugo in to their own home. The overnight stay extended to years as part of Neilly and Rita's family. This raised the number of their family to ten, and Neilly worked hard to provide for all.

In later years when Neilly was in his fifties a study of the health of former surviving Japanese POW was carried out. Neilly was invited to take part. After the war there had been no follow up care or support for those men who had suffered so abominably, and Neilly decided to participate in the study. Even after many years Neilly's blood still carried a record of his time in the camps. The consultant in charge listed the tropical diseases Neilly had suffered, Beri beri, malaria, dengue, fever, dysentery, and a few others. The consultant also noticed that something curious about Neilly's back. Running under the skin was a raised rope like thing. "How long have you had this?" the consultant inquired. "I don't actually know. Do you think that it's anything to do with the time I was in the camps?" Neilly replied. "Indeed I do!" said the doctor. "I think it this is a parasite you caught as a POW, and have been carrying since. It would have been tiny worm, when it first invaded your skin, and over the years it has grown to the size of a small snake" the doctor explained. Thankfully the consultant was able to relieve Neilly of this unpleasant souvenir from the past.

.

With every Joyful moment there is always some sadness

There was also some sadness in Neilly and Rita's' lives, and every New Years day they would visit the grave of the the twin boys they had lost, in 1957. The babies were born at home, as was the custom in those days. The birth was long and difficult. When the baby boys were eventually delivered the infants were feeble and cold. The midwife attending did her best to warm and revive them, with little success. Neilly realising that the boys were slipping away, wrapt the babies in a shawl, and placed them in a holdall bag. There were few telephones in those days, and Neilly did not own a phone or have access to a car. He had no choice but to run with his little sons half a mile to the local maternity home.

Running through the long dark night, as he had done in the camp. Then with the Red Cross parcels to trade for useful items, and now with even more precious cargoes, running for life. Despite all the efforts of the staff at the hospital the little boys died. The babies were baptised and named Peter and Paul. In the early morning light, Neilly returned home now more slowly, carrying his lifeless twin boys.

In the morning when I woke I could see my mother was distressed. When I asked her what was wrong, she told me what had happened. I said nothing, only cried quietly in my room at the awful sadness of it all. My tears were not just for the little lost boys, as even as young child, I could feel my Uncles' pain and the pain of their mother Rita.

Time passed and all the family grew up, intelligent and hard working, each pursuing individual careers. Some law careers, others successful in business, and yet others became skilled tradesmen. Sadly the handsome Owen died young. At only forty four years of age Owen's brain tumour ended his still young life. I remember seeing his son at a family funeral, and as he looked in my direction, I could see he had inherited his father's beautiful shinning green eyes.

Six months earlier Neilly had also lost his lovely Rita. Her death was sudden and not expected, and hit him hard. Neilly and Rita and their twin girls had some years earlier moved to a beautiful old house in the small village of Rhu just outside Helensburgh. The house was surrounded by a large rambling country garden, and an uninterrupted view of the Gareloch.

Now Neilly worked daily in the garden pushing his body to the very limit, as he had done all those years ago, on the Burma Thai railway with Duncan Scrapper Owenie and his other good friends. Now toiling alone, and grieving for Rita. Owenie Burke had passed away some years before his sister. His death was a heavy blow to both Neilly and Rita who never forgot the debt they owed that brave hearted man. While writing about Rita's passing I still feel that I miss my Aunt, who helped make my childhood a happy one, and when I was a young adult with my first few weeks old daughter Kirstin, Rita used her connections in the town of Oban, to enable my family to make our home there. If it had not been for Rita, I may never have moved to the town, and may never, have had such a happy life there.

In time grief eased, and Neilly was to spend a number of happy contented years at the old house in Rhu in the company of his beloved twins Kathleen and Mary. As it neared his eightieth birthday my mother requested that I paint a picture to give to my uncle as a birthday present. It had to be a really special painting. Neilly's eldest son Johnnie had a holiday house in Mullaghduff in Donegal in Ireland, Neilly often holidayed there, and dearly loved this place. I thought this might make a suitable subject. Then I remembered the old cottage which had originally belonged to Neilly's Grandparents, and had eventually become the home of his Father's brother

Hugh and his wife Bridget. Rummaging through boxes of old black and white photographs, I was able to find a number I could use for the painting. The old cottage was there and had myself as a four year old, standing at the door with my Grandfather and Great Uncle Charlie.

Uncle Charlie and Elizabeth

 Seeing this brought back many memories of the two old characters beside me in the photograph. I remembered when I was a young child of four or five; on holiday in Mullaghduff in Ireland my Grandfather's brother Great Uncle Charlie was delighted with his little Great Grand niece. Charlie for some reason had never married, never had had any children of his own, and seemed to be overcome with affection for me. Each day of my stay he would pick me up to hug and kiss me. I did not mind the hugs, but was less fond of the kisses, for Charlie habitually chewed a dried sea weed called dulce. The smell and taste of this lingered in his large moustache! Despite the sea weed kisses I loved the old man dearly, and still have many sweet memories of my Great Uncle Charlie.

I do have some less pleasant memories of my time spent with old Charlie. When I was about seven years of age, Charlie was sitting in the sun outside the old cottage. I was playing with a little black and white kitten nearby. I had made a small bed for the little creature out of a cardboard box, and was stroking and singing a lullaby to the animal which had fallen asleep. I was a soft natured child and loved all the animals around me. Charlie called to me. "Child go to the big house and ask your Aunt Peggy for the knife for the old rooster" The big house was only a few yards from the old cottage, and I skipped happily across the yard to the back door. I pushed the door open and asked my Aunt for the knife. Peggy's eyes widened for a moment. Then she gave me a large long knife from the kitchen drawer, with the firm instruction to walk not run back with the knife to Charlie. I did as she had bid and walked slowly and carefully back to my Uncle, stretched out my arm and offered him the knife. Then I watched him grab the large rooster which had been pecking the dry ground around Charlie's old wooden chair. A few swift movements later he had bent the cockerel's neck and slit the bird's throat. The creature was quickly dead.

Charlie held the bird aloft and blood dripped on to the dry ground below. My brother Terence and cousin Gerard were playing nearby, and came to watch in fascination the death of the poor unfortunate rooster. Charlie then cut off the legs of the dead bird and gave these to the boys, who ran around the farm yard gleefully pulling the tendons of the bird's legs, making them contract and straighten as if the rooster was still alive.

The little child that was me then, stood transfixed. Tears bubbled up in my eyes. I shouted at the boys not to do what they were doing. I hated it, and I hated Charlie as well. He had sent me to go for the knife. Angry and upset I ran away and tried to hide in the cow shed. However there was no sanctuary there. My older cousin young Owenie Boyle was milking the cow, and seeing me crying, called me a bubbly baby, and skilfully directed the cow's teat, to squirt her milk into my already wet eyes.

Charlie had not meant to upset me, indeed he had only wanted to please me and my family. He wanted to give us all a good chicken meal, and these were the days before supermarkets and easily available prepared food.

When I was a little older, and sitting in the kitchen of Auntie Peggy's farm house, Peggy suddenly jumped up from the fireside, and pointing out of the window screamed "Its Charlie the old fool's being dragged through the field by the cow!" Charlie had gone out to the field to take the cow to the barn for milking. He had put a rope around the animal's neck and tried to lead her from the field. However the cow was not in the mood and took off at a fair speed with poor Charlie still hanging on to the end of the rope. We all ran from the kitchen to help. The rescue was the most comical sight. A chain of adults and children hanging on to Charlie and each other, until we had finally brought the bad tempered cow to a halt.

There were other very scary occasions, such as the day Charlie decided to mend the thatch on Aunt Biddy's cottage roof. He propped a very long and rickety old ladder against the gable of the house, and climbed shakily upwards. As he reached the chimney at the height of the ladder, courage failed him, and realising that he was no longer young and fit enough to go through with the roof repairs called out for help. Fortunately I was playing in some sand on the ground near the foot of the ladder. Looking down and seeing me there Charlie cried "Child Go and Fetch your Mother Quickly!" Terrified he would fall to his death, I ran into the cottage to find my Mother also on a ladder trying to repair the storm damage of the day before, and cover up with white distemper paint, the ugly dark stains which the heavy rain had leaked, from the thatched roof, on to the inside of the cottage walls.

My Mother frantically scurried down the indoors ladder, and rushed outside to see poor Charlie on the very wobbly ladder clinging desperately to the cottage chimney. My poor Mum herself afraid of heights, immediately took control of the situation, and after instructing me to steady the bottom of the shaky ladder, bravely mounted the steps and made her way carefully up to the top. There she gently persuaded the trembling Charlie to rung by rung descend to the safety of the ground.

However there were other less traumatic memories of my Great Uncle. The evenings when we all sat round the glowing sweet smelling peat fire and Charlie would entertain all the kids with stories of fairies leprecons and shrieking banshees. If the mood took him Charlie would often burst into song, and I still remember one night when I was about thirteen, and sitting with Charlie and the others sipping tea by the open fire, he without any prompting, out of the blue gave a robust rendition of *The Day We Went to Rothesay 'o*. The whole company fell about in fits of uncontrollable laughter. In hindsight perhaps Charlie was drinking something a little bit stronger than tea.

Neilly's 80th Birthday

Selecting figures from different photographs I composed a picture which showed Neilly's parents standing together at the front of the scene. In the background of the scene, stood the old thatched cottage. Also in the background was a tiny figure bending down to pat a small cat. The finished painting was sent to Helensburgh to be framed.

I was not there when Neilly discovered his painting, for it was not presented to him in the usual manner. Instead the twins hung it on the living room wall and waited for their Father to notice it. This did not take to long, which was just as well, as all the family present, were struggling to hold back their laughter. Neilly was delighted with his present, and then suddenly spotting the small child in the background patting the cat, announced "Look she has put herself in it"

OPERATION PASSPORT

Neilly in 1992 came up against a wall of beaurocracy when he applied to register his Irish birth and obtain an Irish passport. His son Neil wrote the following short story "In the Name of the Faither" depicting the great lengths Neilly had to go to in an attempt to break down the wall, and prove he was Irish and that he existed!

It all started at half time at the Celtic v Porto European Cup-tie at Park head. " Do you fancy going to the away game Neilly?" Big Willie asked the Faither " Ah can get tickets organised. " The Faither seemed agreeable to the prospect of a mid- week sojourn to Portugal. All the Faither had to do was organise a passport, get some Portuguese currency, and learn how to sing "Hail Hail the Celts are here," in Portuguese. The Faither a sprightly eighty three year old season ticket and shareholder at Celtic Park, very seldom misses a home game. Mr Celtic. The Faither didnae need much persuasion!
"I'll mention to the twins tonight " thought the Faither, " and maybe they will help take care of the arrangements" Celtic won the first leg 1-0. If Celtic won or drew the away leg they would be favourites to progress to the next stages of the Champions League. The Faither was already looking forward to the trip.

"They have done away with visitors passports!" advised the sister who had taken on board the arrangements. You'll need to apply for a full passport. "All we need to do is fill in the form, get your photo taken, and send it away with a cheque together with your birth certificate. You'll get a passport back in the post. You will enjoy Portugal, the Celts did O.K. in Portugal in 1967!" said the sister who knew a thing or two about fitba." Only O.K. thought the Faither. "Sure we won the European Cup in Lisbon in 1967."

"There might be a wee problem!" indicated the Faither, with a sheepish look on his face. "Ah've no got a birth certificate ! " Any time your Mammy and me went abroad, we went on Visitor Passport which was issued at the local Post Office. Everyone knew who we were, so we had no bother getting one. " But you must have a birth certificate , surely. " suggested the brother. "Naw I've never had one. I don't think your Granda registered me in either Ireland or Scotland" replied the Faither. I know I was born in Mullaghduff in County Donegal in Ireland on the 4th of December 1918. Your Granny and Granda told me that. I was baptized in St Mary's Kinncasslagh the next day. They used to speak about my Auntie Annie Eoin who had the wee tin shop next to the old house, carrying me in a shawl, and walking through miles of snow to get me baptized! They say I was poorly at the time, but there was no mention of rushing me to a doctor. Aye they had their priorities right in the old days! Years later we heard in a letter from Uncle Charlie Eoin, that there was a fire in the church in Kinncasslagh, and all the records were burned!

So Iv'e got neither a birth certificate nor a baptismal certificate.

The Faither was born in Mullaghduff although his five sisters were born in Helens burgh in Scotland. The Granda, John Eoin Rua, who was from Donegal, was in the British Navy during the first world war. When the rebellion broke out in Dublin at Easter 1916 the Granda along with thousands of Irishmen jumped ship, and made his way back to Ireland. The greatest war was at home! The British navy was bombarding Dublin with shells, and troops were on the streets. Britain was at war against Ireland. There was no way Granda was fighting for Britain under these circumstances! "Home Boys Home!"

The penalty for desertion was death. My Granny and Granda moved from Helens burgh in Scotland to the Rosses Donegal, along with their two daughters Annie and Gracie. It was during this period in Ireland that the red haired Faither was born. When the British Government granted an amnesty to Irishmen who returned to their ranks the Granda gave himself up. I don't know how it happened, but he ended up in the British Army, enlisted in the Enniskillen Fusiliers. The Granda was wounded during the war and at the conclusion of the hostilities returned to his family in Mullaghduff. Six weeks after the Faither's birth, the family returned to Scotland, where another three sisters Mary Sadie and Patsy were born.

So there was the Faither six weeks old born in Ireland living in Scotland, nae birth certificate. Now here was the Faither born in Ireland, living in Scotland, nearly eighty three years later, and still nae birth certificate! Nothing much had changed. The pace was just about right. No rush. Take your time. Sure you get there just the same! Donegal is renowned for its laid back attitude. The brother said "Apparently there are over twenty words in the Gaelic language equivalent to the Spanish word manana, but noone of them are as urgent!"

The sister contacted Birth Deaths and Marriages in Dublin, who referred her to Letterkenny. An application would require to be made to register the Faither's birth late. Nearly eighty three years late! But sure things never go to quickly in Donegal. Births Deaths and Marriages (Hatches, Matches and Despatches Uncle Owenie had called them) said that the Faither would have to prove he existed! The Faither had worked since the age of fourteen, paid tax all his working life, had a National Insurance Number, had Army Discharge Papers (honourable), had spent years in Japanese POW camps, had Old age and War Pension but they wanted proof that he existed! The Faither was also Father to nine children, seven boys and twin girls. If the Faither didnae exist whit did that make them? "I've often been called a wee bastard" quipped the brother. The Faither gave a disapproving look. "Well maybe we are nine wee Immaculate Conceptions? Continued the brother, just think what it would do for the Rosses if they discovered that we were nine wee Immaculate Conceptions. The place would be jumping! They could shut Knock down!" The brother was getting in deeper. If the Faither didnae exist who was that who used to lift us over the turnstile at Celtic Park?" asked the other brother, trying to steer the brother out of trouble. "It's just Rid Tape gone mad!" suggested the other brother.

The Porto game in the meantime had come and gone. Celtic were defeated 2-0. The Faither was glad he had missed the game, but had the bit between his teeth now. He was determined to get a passport. He would prove he existed all right. The Faither had to produce supporting evidence that he existed, and had to swear a declaration before an Irish Commissioner for the Peace. I was thinking the Faither might be swearing very soon! The sister drew up an action plan. Visit St Mary's Church in Kinncasslagh, and get whatever information we could from the local priest, contact Births Deaths and Marriages in Letterkenny. Swear the declaration. Get the application advanced as far as we could. Operation passport was underway! Telephone contact would be kept between Rhu and Mullaghduff.

Donegal here we come. We are on the One Road. The Faither and the three brothers set off from Helensburgh at seven thirty in the morning. Following the River Clyde, we travelled through Dumbarton, Clydebank, Glasgow, and before we knew it we were driving through Rabbie Burns Country in Ayrshire heading for Stranraer and Larne Ferry. Paddy's Milestone, or the Ailsa Craig, to give it it's Sunday name, appeared out of the sea in front of us, then behind us, and then in front of us again. We stopped in Girvan for bridies. Noreen the neighbour in Donegal used to live in Glasgow and misses the bridies with the onions in them, which you can't buy in Donegal. On arrival at Stranraer the brother treated us all to a Roll and sausage, or a roll and bacon, a mug of coffee and we were all set for the two hour sea journey to Larne.

The boat journey was uneventful, a smooth crossing. We settled in the quiet lounge reading newspapers and drinking coffee. The brother who had been driving dozed off and began to snore loudly. "Quiet Please! Quiet Please! We are in the Quiet Lounge!" I rebuked. No response, Snore, Snore! "Quite Please" I repeated. No response! The Faither gave the snoring brother a wee dig in the ribs. Silence. No more snoring! The Quiet man in the Quiet Lounge. "Even a wee dig from the Faither would be quite sore" suggested the other brother, "Ah'm no going to sleep in case ah snore!" By the time I had read the newspaper and made a miserable attempt at the crossword, we were sailing into Larne harbour. County Antrim beckoned.

We disembarked, passed through security and the brother's car was sprayed for foot and mouth contamination. The brother cracked some joke about banning Orange parades, because of "Flute and mouth" but it was an old one. We were soon driving through Larne, Dungiven, and over the River Foyle at Derry. The brother was eating up the miles. Soon we would be over the border and into Donegal. A stop in Letterkenny to recharge the batteries. Then had home-made soup and fresh sandwiches in the Colorado

Café next door to the auctioneers. There were three rifles mounted on the wall of the Colorado Café. The brother said he was satisfied that they had been put beyond use, and tucked into the grub.

We had the usual conversation in Letterkenny about whether to go via Finntown and Doochray and up the Corkscrew, or to go through the National Park. "The Finntown roads are better but the Glen road is a bit quicker" thought the brother. "When you get this far you just want to be there!" We decided to take the Glenveigh route. Darkness was beginning to fall and the rain did not look too far away." It disnae half get dark quick over here!" observed the brother as we headed out of Letterkenny. We passed through Kilmacrenan where big Pat and Deirdre had the house. Big Pat was now buried there. A shortcut through the beautiful Glenveigh National Park.

There was a slight delay because they were repairing the roads. The road had been in the process of being upgraded for the past ten years. Now the upgrading needed upgraded . Every now and then a sheep, sometimes two or three would wander aimlessly in front of the car. " Sheep's eyes instead of cats eyes they have over here" joked the brother. Nobody laughed! We passed the Glenveigh Inn where we had stopped on the way back from Peggy's funeral, and missed the boat back home. We passed the poisoned Glen with it's roofless church, and onto Dunlewey under the shadow of mount Errigal.

"Can you smell the beautiful burning peat? Asked the Faither. "You know you we've not far to go now you can smell the turf." Left at the crossroads, down through Crolly, Annagry to Bunnaman where Granny's people are said to come from. Minutes later we were driving through Calhame, where Granny's people are said to come from as well. A stone sign at the roadside told us we had arrived in the lovely Mullach Dhu or Mullaghduff where the Faither was born. Home!

The brother was soon indicating to turn right at Murray's shop and driving up the cassan to his house on the hill on Drimrua Mullaghduff. The shop was still called Murray's and always would be referred to as Murray's, although Murray had long since passed on. The same applied to the local pubs which were still referred to locally by the names of long deceased former owners. It is just the way. Our destination was the brother's cottage. When the brother was planning his retirement he bought an idyllic cottage which is equidistant from the two village pubs.

The house on the hill called Drimrua
What a view! What a wonderful sight!
Bonner's sits just to the left
Neddie's sits just to the right!

The views from the hill are really amazing. The house looks onto the Rannyhual mountain on one side, and on to the Atlantic Ocean on the other. Looking East,

Mount Errigal, the highest mountain in Donegal, is clearly in view, like an old man with its grey headed peak. The Islands of Gola, Innesfree, Owey, Rutland, and Arranmore, can be viewed in the distance. Part of the brother's land is bordered by a beautiful dark lake called Lough Naweeloge. Peace and serenity, Heaven on Earth. One of the neighbours, Patrick Frank Neil who has spent almost ninety years on the hill, pointed out that four different parishes can be viewed from Drimrua. The Atlantic breakers can be seen smashing off the Stags or the Na Mhic Uag Corra, the Gaelic name for three rocks which protrude from the Atlantic. Local legend has it that these rocks were in fact human who were turned into rock by St Columcile. The rocks are named Tadhg, Brian, and Una. On the 1st of May each year the rocks are said to take human form again, and swim towards the shore, but if they are viewed by a human eye, they immediately revert to stone! I was wondering if they had birth certificates!

When we arrived, the neighbours Hughie and Noreen had a turf fire blazing and the kettle on the boil. We were quickly settled round the turf fire supping mugs of tea. "Nothing strange sure things are just the same" was Hughie's summary of the goings on, since the last time we had visited a few months previously. Noreen was now a redhead and was going to the gym a few days a week! "Maybe she has another part in a film" I was thinking. I would ask her later. The other neighbour Mary brought up a scone which she had baked for the Faither. We were home.

The scone, smothered in delicious home made blackberry jam, which the Faither's cousin had sent up, didn't stand a chance, and was quickly devoured by the hungry travellers. Operation passport was on schedule, and having arrived at the Faither's birthplace, we reported back to the sisters in Rhu.

And soon we'll be arriving at a place we call home
See familiar places, where in boyhood we did roam
Meet the friends and relations
Pass the news and have the craic
It is the people and the welcome
That always brings me back.

Next day the neighbour, Patrick Frank Neil, one of the oldest landmarks around here as Thomas had once referred to him, gave the Faither the history of the Kinncasslagh parish. St Mary's Kinncasslagh, part of the parish of lower Templecrone, was once served from the parish church at Acres. The parish priest was resident there, and would travel on horseback to the other churches to say Mass. "Maybe there would be baptismal records at Burtonport from them days" suggested wee Patrick. The parish of lower Templecrone was then divided in 1945 and now consists of two parishes, Annagry and Kinncasslagh. Patrick explained the boundaries of the parishes to the Faither, and pointed out that the dividing line was the wee burn at the bottom of the road! After the history lesson the Faither was satisfied that he had been baptized in Kinncasslagh, which would be the parish of Mullaghduff at the time.

We made contact with the local priest at Kinncasslagh after Mass on Sunday. The young bright faced priest with a well fed look about him, invited us in to the Sacristy. The brother explained the Faither's predicament to the Father. The priest was a bit bemused that a near 83 year old man would go to all this bother to see the Celtic. The priest confirmed that many Church records had been destroyed by fire.

"It was in this very room the fire took place in 1927" explained the sandaled priest. "The loss of baptismal, marriage and death records, has caused confusion over the years. The usual enquiry is for death records, but I cannot recall anyone looking for birth records to enable them to go abroad to watch the Celtic before. Fair play to you, I'll see what I can do. You don't look like you would be one of Bin Laden's men" joked the priest. I was thinking that with the beard and sandals the priest looked a more likely candidate. "If he wasn't so fair featured, and he had a rocket launcher on his shoulder, sure you could mistake him for the Taliban" I was thinking.

"Come up to the Chapel house after 10.00 o'clock Mass tomorrow morning" suggested the priest. "I'll speak to some priests who have experienced such requests before, and see what we can do to help you in your quest to see the Celtic" "Mass two days in a row! That's one way to increase the congregation" I was thinking, and I was thinking my brother was thinking that as well. Next day after Mass the priest phoned Births Deaths and Marriages in Letterkenny.

It turned out that the assistant in the office was from Mullaghduff. She was Francie Mickie Eoin's granddaughter, and she would help us complete the application. We thanked the very helpful priest, and were immediately headed for Letterkenny.

When we arrived at B.D.+ M. there was a couple with a young baby already in the small cramped waiting room. The Father was in his forties, a new age type, cool, long hair and beard, child in papoose around his neck, and staring lovingly into the newborn child's eyes. Your man was enjoying Fatherhood. "Goo! Goo!" He gooed. "Are you here to register tour daughter's birth? I asked the proud father. "My son's birth corrected the hippy. " He is lovely" I muttered apologetically. "Yes we are here to register young Damien- Zac's birth" said the new age father. "We are here on the same mission" I offered. We are here to register the birth of this fella here" and nodded over to the corner where the Faither was seated, shiny faced, smiling, Donegal tweed bunnet lying in his lap. The new age father was really tickled with the story about the Faither's attempts to prove his existence and wished the Faither luck. It was cool!
Angela, the girl in the office, invited the Faither and the brother into a wee ante-room to complete the application form. The brother introduced the Faither to Angela and said" I think we could nearly be related" Sure the brother was right enough. The Faither's cousin Owenie's daughter Grace Owenie is married to Anthony Peggy, the son of Peggy Mickie Owen, who is the sister of Francie Mickie Owen, whose son is Angela's father, making her Francie Mickie

Owen's granddaughter. Not really a close relation. But close enough! A wee bit of nepotism never goes amiss! I had once heard another brother saying to Thomas, "Aye if you threw a stone in Mullaghduff, you would likely hit a relation" Maybe the brother was about right!

Soon after the brother and the Faither went into the room, music suddenly came blasting through the speakers on the wall. " Maybe they are giving the Faither a music test" suggested the other brother. "Maybe they are being interrogated and the music is to drown the screams" He further postulated. "Customer Care?" The brother and me couldn't hear a single word that was being said through the wall!

The waiting room got busy again as another young couple, babe in arms, came in to register the birth. I didn't want to risk getting the gender wrong this time and just remarked "Aye your child is really lovely" and proffered the advice "register the birth early and save a lot of trouble in later years. We could learn from you young bucks". "Good advice . Good advice" I could see the brother thinking, as the young mother gave me a funny sort of look. The Faither and the brother came out of the office smiling. Angela the relation had been very helpful and had part completed the form ready for a signature by a commissioner of the peace. She had also given the Faither the names and addresses of a few Commissioners. We would deal with that tomorrow. We were already getting in to the Donegal pace. Angela had also suggested that

we try to get a copy of the Granny and Granddad's marriage certificate to support the application.
We would contact the twins tonight and ask them to try and obtain the marriage lines.

A visit to St Josephs, Helensburgh followed by a visit to the registrar's office, and the sister had the extract of the Grandparent's marriage certificate. The Granny's maiden name was Sharkey and her mother's name had been McKenzie. The Faither's Grandfather Sharkey had been called Neil. The Granda's father had been Eoin Rua and his mother Grace Sweenie. Grace, Neil, and Eoin or Owen are popular names in the family with each of the names appearing at least once in the last four generations.
"It's great what you can glean from an old document" said the brother. " We'll need to start a family tree."
There will be a few branches on that tree alright

There's McGinley's and Sharkeys there's Boyles here too
Duffys, Rodgers and Bonners
To name just a few
The O'Donnells were the Kings
In Tir Connail's old land
Down in old Mullaghduff by Mullaghderg strand.

The last piece of the jig-saw was complete, and it was now just a matter of getting the declaration sworn, and sending the application, and supporting documents, to Dublin for consideration.

We were directed to the Commissioner of the Peace in Annagry, John Mickie Boyle the painter. The Commissioner invited the Faither and the brother into his home. When the situation was explained John Mickie without any pomp or ceremony he asked " Where do I sign?" The document having been duly authenticated, the Commissioner wished the Faither and the Celtic the very best on their travels.

Word travels fast in Mullaghduff and when we went to Neddies pub at night the locals were interested to hear about the progress of Operation Passport. Bubbles Boyle a retired civil servant, back living in Mullaghduff, was quick to offer the Faither advice. "Neilly" She said. " there's plenty of old fellas your age buried down in Kinncasslagh cemetery. Sure all you have to do is go down and get their details from the gravestone and apply for the certificate in their name. You wouldn't be doing anything wrong as these fellas won't be needing a passport!" "But it's a birth certificate I'm after Bubbles" explained the Faither. "Not a death certificate." "Och, well I know Neilly" replied Bubbles " but you will get enough details from the death certificate to apply for the birth certificate. It's been done before. "Even better Neilly" the ginger haired Bubbles said to the Faither. "Make an application for three State pensions." "Three?" questioned the Faither. "Aye three" answered the retired civil servant." If you apply for three pensions you can be feckin sure that they will find out very quickly exactly who you are! They'll even tell you the name of the midwife!" chuckled Bubbles. "The craic was fierce" as they say.

On the day before we left Donegal, mission almost accomplished, we visited the Kerry town shrine, where Our Lady is said to have appeared. I couldn't help wondering what Mammy would have made of Operation Passport. I'm sure she would have approved, and in my mind, I could hear her say "Whit a lot of palaver!" "Aye he bloody exists all right!" I had a wee smile to myself.

The application has been sent to Dublin, and the Faither is now patiently awaiting the decision of the Irish Government! It doesn't look like the Faither will be travelling abroad to see the Celts in Europe this season. I'm just hoping and praying that the bureaucrats see sense, and accept that the Faither does exist, and that it's not to long until the little green passport with the gold harp on the front pops through Faither's letter box! Otherwise my next wee story may be "The travels of an 83 year old illegal immigrant Celtic supporter"

'IN THE NAME OF THE FAITHER'
(the sequel)

The Irish Harp on the back of the envelope had the Faither's heart beating a wee bit faster. The Faither put on the glasses. With a steady hand, the Faither opened the envelope from the Registrar of Births Deaths and Marriages in Dublin. After our trip to Ireland, the sister had sent off all the documents, which had been suggested, together with the application for registration of birth to the Office of Births Deaths and Marriages in Dublin.

'It will be the long awaited late registration of the my birth.' thought the Faither 'The application would take 12 weeks to process' the sister had been advised by the office in Letterkenny. Fourteen weeks had now elapsed.
'Sure if I've waited almost 84 years now I don't suppose we'll fall out over another 12 weeks' accepted the Faither.
The Faither put the letter down on the table. He changed his glasses and read the letter. The application had been refused. No reason given. Insufficient evidence of birth in Ireland. Cheque returned.
The Faither was flabbergasted. When it sunk that the application had been refused the Faither was

beelin. 'Widyoubelieveit? They have knocked back my application! 'Widyoubelieveit?'

'Aye the green stuff seems to be a bit tighter than the red stuff

Alright' suggested the brother.

The official government letter ended 'if you have any inquiries about this reply do not hesitate to call the above number.'

The Faither took the letter literally. He did not hesitate.

After about five attempts at mastering the telephone code to Dublin,

the Faither was through to the correct Department.

'No I'd like to speak to your boss.'

'I'm sorry my boss is busy' said the apologetic Assistant 'I'll see if he is free.'

'I'm not putting the phone down until I speak to the man in charge.' replied the Faither digging in his heels.

The Faither was put on hold, listening to Beethoven.

After about a quarter of an hour of classical music, the Faither was through to the top cookie in B D &Mt

'Nice music you have.'

The Faither introduced himself, and once again explained his predicament Born in Ireland on 4th December 1918! Baptized in Ireland on 5 December 1918; No birth certificate; baptismal records burned in a fire in the chapel in Kinncasslagh in 1927; a copy of the Granny and Granda's Marriage certificate; school records; National Insurance records; tax records; Army records; POW records; records of the pension. Every conceivable record except the record of my birth.

Cannot get a passport without a birth certificate; Need a Passport to see Celtic abroad.
'Can you not make an old man happy? pleaded the Faither.'
Naw, the Faither disnae plead, soft soap maybe, but no plead, you know what I mean.
'No I am sorry there is nothing in the supporting documents which allows me to make the presumption that you were born in Ireland' was the civil servant's curt reply. 'In fact the evidence would lean more towards you being born in Scotland.' continued the cheeky bastard.
This was anathema to the Faither. Like a red rag to a bull. A red headed bull! It was just as well this was a phone call, and not face to face. The Faither's face was reddening.
'What are you trying to tell me? I'm the man from Godknowswhere?
Spluttered the Faither. 'Are you saying I'm John Doe? Are you telling me I don't exist? You are denying me my birthright! You are saying I'm not Irish! I've been Irish since the day I was born, and proud to be Irish.' The Faither's dander was getting up.
'I'm sorry there is nothing I can do further to assist? Said the uncivil servant, trying to terminate the call. Don't think for a minute that you've heard the end of this. I've got contact with several T.D.s. There will be questions asked in the Dail!
You'll be reading about this in the newspapers!'
The Faither would be talking to his contacts. Pat the Cope would be hearing about this. The Faither would

be writing to Bertie. the top cookie in BD&M was listening.

'Well if you could get sworn statements from people who remember your birth in Mullaghduff ... er... maybe...' compromised the civil servant.

'But I'm almost 84. I don't think there will be too many folk in Muilaghduff, who would have been around, at the time of my birth.

I'm sure I could obtain statements from relations and friends who know from their parents of my birthplace.

'Perhaps that would assist' conceded the Dub.

The Faither had the bit between the gums now!

'When you have the Affidavits sworn and a statement from the Parish Priest that the records were destroyed I'll reconsider your application.'

Round one to the Faither. The Green stuff was loosening a bit.

I've been Irish since the day I was born
I'm as Irish Sir as you
As Irish as the hills of Donegal
As Irish as Brian Buru
Me Faither Sir, before me
His Faither and His faither too
Each and every one of us
Was born in Mullagh Dhu!

'Affy David? Who the feck is Affy David?'

'Naw. Affidavit. It's a legal word for a sworn statement. The Faither is wanting us to get them sworn and signed when we're over in Donegal next week.'

'I bet the Faither was swearing when he was told the application was refused.'

'We have to get statements from the relations saying they know who the Faither is and that he was born in Donegal. Maybe one from Francie Mickie Eoin and his sister Peggy as well.'

'Ah thought Affy David was one of those Donegal names like Hughie Danny Francie and the like' ' Are you winding me up? We've to get a letter from the priest stating that the records were burned in a fire in the Church in
Kinncasslagh as well.'

'That's to make sure we go to chapel! Three times we went on the last visit.'

' The wee priest in Kinncasslagh doesnae hang about. He says a quick Mass.'

'No as fast as Father Zorro. He once said a Mass in the time it takes a pint of Guinness to settle.'

'Aye, Fr. Pat is a cheery wee priest and he was really helpful the last time we explained the Faither's situation. Mind he was kidding the Faither about Bin Ladin. I'm certain he'll do the necessary.'

'We shouldn't have any bother getting the documents signed.

Then I'm sure the wee painter who acts as Commissioner for the Peace will authenticate them, nae problem.'

They tried too say he wisnae Irish
He said I'm Irish through and through
He got signed and sworn statements
From the good folk of Mullaghdhu
And other folk who knew him
And knew his kith and kin
The Faither would prove his claim
The Faither he would win

' Welcome Home. How's things going with your father's passport?' These were the first words from Annie in the wee shop at the bottom of the cassan on our arrival in Mullaghduff. The wee shop had served the community for generations. The Faither's Aunt Annie, his Godmother, ran a similar wee shop at the other end of the townland when she was alive.
The brother gave Annie and the queue, which had built up, an update on the Faither's continuing quest for recognition as an Irishman.
'He canny sing 'when Irish Eyes are Smiling' wae a straight face!' threw in the brother.
Francie Mickie Eoin was in the queue. 'Sure I've known your father all his life. Who is this who is saying he's not Irish? Sign a statement? I'll do better than that. I'll write a letter to Dublin telling them I know your Dad is Irish. I'm only six months older than

your Father but as far back as I can recall, your Father has been coming back and forward to Mullaghduff. Sure everyone around here knows that he was born here. I remember his father John Eoin and his mother Mary. Sure the shed that Neilly was born in still stands at the back of our house. Not a doubt about it. Neilly John Eoin was born in Mullaghduff.' Strike while the iron is hot. The brother got the Affidavit signed.

'A loaf and a pint of milk Annie.'

Francie's sister Peggy Mickie Eoin was equally adamant about the Faither's place of birth. 'He was born right here in Mullaghduff. Neilly is as Irish as the Banshee Stone at Mullagh Derg. I'll show you the hut out the back where he was born. It has a proper roof now but it was thatched
then. You can still see where the bed would be in the corner. I can remember well your Granny and Granda coming Home each year, remember all your Dad's sisters. We looked forward to them coming home on holiday. There was Annie, she came the most. Her son Frankie went out with a few Mullaghduff girls when he was here on holiday. He broke a few hearts. Then there was Grade, Mary, Sadie and the youngest was Patsy, if I'm remembering right. Patsy came over with her children in later years. Then I can remember your Father and Mother bringing all you crowd over on holiday as well. Everyone brought their family at one time. It was always busy around in them days.'

The brother got Peggy Mickie Eoin to sign the Affidavit but missed out the bit about the bed in the corner and the Banshee Stone.

The Faither's cousins Anthony Dora and Brid Dora were upset when the brother related the sad tale and the Faither's anguish at being dubbed 'the man from Godknowswhere' by the Irish Government. The brother was milking the story dry. The Post Office in Annagry which the Faither's cousin ran had been in the family since 1884. 'If they paid family allowance in your father's day we could check the records back, that would have been proof that your father was from here.' suggested the cousin. The cousins both knew from their parents and family history that the Faither was a Mullaghduffman. The affidavits were duly signed.

Ownie Boyle, the Faither's other cousin is a hard man to get a hold of now that he has retired. He is never in. After a few unsuccessful attempts at catching the gentleman farmer, the brothers left the paperwork for signature. The next day the Faither's cousin's daughter, Grace Owenie delivered the affidavit signed by Owenie and authenticated *by* the brother in law who is a Commissioner in Glenties, a position he inherited from his father. The Commissioner has a bold name plate outside his house in Glenties.
' Sure Neilly can shift that owd whiskey like a Mullaghduffman' praised Grace Owenie. 'Do you want that in a statement?' 'Scotsmen have been

known to shift the whisky as well Gracie' informed the brother. ' That doenae make them Irish.'

'Sure, Thomas would have been the man to write a statement about your father's history, alright.' suggested Gracie.

' Aye! Thomas could have told the whole of Mullaghduff their histories' agreed the brother.'

St. Mary's Church, Kinncasslagh, deep in the heart of 'Daniel Country', was the next port of call for the brothers.

The wee priest in Kinncasslagh remembered the brothers from the last visit. 'No problem boys. I'll type out a letter stating that you father's baptismal records were burned. I've entered your father's details in a register I am trying to compile to replace the burned records.' The priest guided the brothers into a large lounge. " Take a seat boys.' The remnants of a hearty breakfast sat on the coffee table.' 'We are not interrupting your breakfast Father, are we?' 'No, not at all. Sure it's after two o'clock!'

'I noticed a sign outside a pub in Dungloe advertising all day breakfasts. I was thinking you must be an all day breakfast man, Father.' quipped the brother.

' All day breakfast? No I finished my breakfast hours ago.' said the priest wiping the egg yolk from his mouth. 'I'll type the letter right away. I'll be back in a minute.'

'It's nae wonder the wee priest remembered us. We were here three times in the one week, last time.'

The brothers could hear the sound of the sandaled priest's one-fingered click click.... click on the typewriter through in his study.

'Are you sending it in Morse code Father?' joked the brother quietly enough for the priest not to hear him. Click ....click ....click echoed through the Chapel House.

'Do you remember when we were over for Hudie's funeral. When we were following the coffin, an old woman in black grabbed the Faither's arm, looked into his eyes and said 'Owenie Mhor is still alive' referring to the resemblance between the Faither to his uncle.' 'Aye, it was a wee bit scary.'

'I remember Mammy telling us about one time they were in Mullaghduff overhearing someone say ' I don't know who he is, but he must one of the people. He looks like one of the people 'Aye and they are still saying he isnae Irish!' Click...click...click

'How would we know or care about Mullaghduff on the edge of the Atlantic if we didnae have the Faither's connection with the place?'

' Can you think of any reason why a man would take his wife and nine weans, aged between one and twelve on an overnight boat from Glasgow to Derry travelling steerage, followed by a bumpy journey through the winding mountain roads of Donegal to visit the hamlet of Mullaghduff?'

'If a man was born there and had a love of his birth place would he not maybe make such a journey?'

'You don't have to convince me but you should put that bit in an Affey Davie.'

'You should tell them about the MuHaghduff midges, in an Affey Davie as well' suggested the brother. Click click click.

'The Mullaghduff Midge' is an almost invisible little mite known colloquially as 'a wee fecker' and is reputed to only bite strangers.

Unless you were born in Mullashduff you are a stranger. When the Faither, the sisters, the brother and the wife were Home in the summer, 'the wee feckers' mounted an airborne attack. Everyone was covered in swollen, itchy blotches except the Faither. 'That surely proves something.'

'Aye, the Faither is thick-skinned.'

'We'll maybe tell Dublin about the Mullaghduff midges anyway.'

'Do you think the Faither will talk wae an Irish accent if he gets his Irish birth certificate?"

'Sure the brother speaks wae wan when he's here for a week!' The Click....click....clicking from the priest's study suddenly stopped.

Father Pat, looking pleased with his handiwork, presented the brothers with a signed letter on Church headed notepaper and stamped with the diocesan stamp. The letter certified that the Faither's baptismal records were lost in a fire in St. Marys Church, Kinncasslagh in 1925.

'Aye you are a dab hand at the old typing Father.' peeheed the brother.

The bureaucrat in Dublin would be impressed. As good as the Papal seal. The brothers thanked the priest and hoped he enjoyed the rest of his breakfast.

In the evening, the brothers paid their customary visit to Neddies, the local pub.
NONE of your 'What would you like to drink?' Jimmie the landlord's opening line was 'How did your Dad get on with his passport?' Jimmie had given the Faither a few old books which recorded the Granda and his brother's service in the Great War. The Granda's brother, James Eoin was killed in action in Gallipoli. The Granda was also shot, but he survived.
The brother gave Jimmie and the bar an update of the Faither's passport pursuit, adding wee bits on here and there. He had a listening audience.
'How could anyone doubt that the Faither was Irish? He told them about the flag which the Faither's pal Shaney had painted him during the War. The flag was pinned above the Faither's bed in the barracks of the Argyll and Sutherland Highlanders which was not renowned for being a particularly Tim regiment. After a drink some soldiers, including a big orangeman from the Vale of Leven would take umbrage to the flag. He told them about the Faither defending his Erin Go Bragh flag above his bed from the orangeman from the Vale. The flag remained above the bed. The brother didn't tell them about the Faither giving the Valeman a fried kipper in Burma. That's another story.
'The Boyos who got caught train spotting in Columbia were traveling on false passports. They are not hard to come by, you know.' Offered the man in the corner sipping Guinness.
' I know a few train spotters who might be able to help.'

'The Faither was declaring he was Irish on Ministry of Defence Security forms at a job in Glen Douglas when Irishmen, new over, were declaring themselves British for fear of discrimination. He was Irish when it was sometimes easier not to be.'
'If any of you were half decent at football it would solve your father's
problem suggested Frankie Pat, 'Big Mick would get your father a birth certificate alright and would have you playing for Ireland in jig time!'
The brother told them that we already had an established footballer in the family. He told them about the Faither representing Ireland against Scotland in a football match in the POW camp. There was a Captain Boyle played for Scotland. How could they even suggest the Faither wisnae Irish?

'I'd rather have someone in the team who want's to be Irish and wants to play. No like that spoiled big shite Keane.' was thrown in for the benefit of Ronan who was the only man in Mullaghduff apart from the Yank who was defending the ex-Irish captain. 'The craic was fierce.' as they say.
'Write to the newspapers, that will get them jumping!' suggested Bubbles Boyle. Bubbles had previously suggested using details from a dead man's gravestone to apply for a passport. 'Sure I was in the Sunday People with my dogs Larsson and Sutton last week. And Daniel and Packie are in the

Sun this week wearing bras, your father's story would get in the papers.'

'The Faither's desperate to get a passport Bubbles, but I don't think he would go as far as wear a bra.'

The brother would be talking to the journalist if the application was refused. He has already briefed him. The last time the journalist was let loose in Donegal his article about Donegal farmers and sheep caused a scandal. The Donegal TD was ridiculed in the Dail. The article wasn't about foot and mouth

There was not one in the pub who doubted the Faither's Irishness. 'Sure you can tell just by looking at your father that he is from here.

You just know it.' The brother could have got a hundred Affy Davids.

The next job on the brothers' list was to get the deeds authenticated by the painter and Commissioner for the Peace, John Mickie Boyle.

'There's an awful lot of Boyles involved in this mission' the brother was thinking.

The brothers didn't get a chance to introduce themselves. The Commissioner remembered them and welcomed them into his home. They had only met once when the Faither swore the declaration before him the previous year. The brothers didn't know that the Faither's cousin had announced their impending arrival, the minute they had left the Post Office and had updated the Commissioner with the Faither's plight.

'Come in. Sit down. I heard yous were about. It will be about your Father wanting to see the Celtic. Sure I remember you fine. This man will have to get to see the Celtic abroad. Where do you want me to sign? The Affidavits were countersigned by John Mickie. Totally informal. No pomp or ceremony Donegal style. The brothers were wishing that John Mickie was the top cookie in Births deaths and Marriages.

The signed and authenticated documents were submitted to the B D&M in Dublin by the sister along with the application for registration, and the original supporting documents.
'We'll have to wait another 12 weeks while they consider the application again.' the sister informed the Faither.
'What is there to consider? Surely when he reads the statements he will be satisfied.' 'No they said twelve weeks.'
'If we don't hear in twelve weeks we'll get right back onto them. The season has started and the Champions League will be starting soon.'
The Faither's patience was being sorely tested.

'I can assure you I personally posted the documents to you over twelve weeks ago' said the sister in an annoyed voice. 'I'm sorry we have no record of having received them.' The sister informed the civil servant of the trouble we had all gone to obtain the documents.

She told them that the Faither was getting anxious about the application. 'Yes, I appreciate you have gone to great trouble to get these documents, including two visits to Ireland.' 'I have retained copies of the documents which I will fax to you immediately.'
'As soon as they arrive I will place the faxed copies before my boss for consideration.'
'It won't take another twelve weeks will it?'
'No please phone back tomorrow, I hope to have an answer for you .'
The green stuff was loosening a wee bit more.

The Sister phoned Dublin the next day. No Beethoven. She was put straight through to the top cookie.
'Really, Affidavits are not evidence' bullshitted the cheeky bastard. 'It was yourself who suggested that we get them!'
'Oh, I see there is one here from an 84 year old Francie Mickie Eoin That helps. And here is one from his sister. What does she say now' Oh, she knows the house your father was born in? 'Can you not get a copy of your Father's baptismal certificate?' the dim-witted bureaucrat asked.
An exasperated sister explained that the baptismal records had been lost in a Church fire and, that as requested by him, we had obtained a certificate from the local priest to that effect,
'I faxed a copy to your assistant yesterday. 'Why does it take twelve weeks and here is the application being

considered over the phone?' 'Oh yes I see. Yes. I've got it here. That helps as well. Because of the great bother you have gone to in pursuit of your registration I am prepared to look on the application favorably.' concluded tin bureaucrat grudgingly.' I'm sure he didn't want the Faither on the phone again! ' I will write to you with an official reply in a few days.' Round two to the Faither. The green stuff was almost loose.

The Irish Harp on the back of the envelope had the Faither's heart beating a wee bit faster. The Faither put on the glasses.The Faither with a steady hand, opened the long awaited envelope from the Registrar of Births Deaths and Marriages in Dublin. 'Surely it will be good news this time.' the Faither was thinking.
The Faither put the letter on the table and changed his glasses.
Inside was a certificate of registration of the Faither's birth.
The application for late registration had been granted, Donegal style. Almost 84 years late! Sure what's the rush!
The certificate signed by the Superintendent Registrar of Births Deaths and Marriages, St. Joseph's Hospital, Stranorlor, certified that the Faither was born in Mullaghduff on 4 December 1918 and that his birth was now entered in the registers for the Registration District of Dungloe, Co. Donegal.

Game set and match to the Faither! The green tape was off completely The Faither is an Irishman. It's official!

The Faither didnae take no for an answer
The government were in for a fight
I'm Irish! Said the Faither
You won't deny my birthright
I'm Irish said the Faither
I shall not be moved
The bureaucrats at last saw sense
The application was approved.

A delighted Irish Faither applied for the passport on Monday and Celtic went out of the Champions League on Wednesday.

'Have passport will travel'… addendum to the sequel to the name of the Faither

'We'll need to send away for a passport now that you are a fully fledged Irishman Dad' suggested the sister. 'Aye' said the Faither 'and I'll maybe get to a European game next season, the Bhoys are well on their way to winning the league again this year'
There was no delay this time and the passport arrived within a few weeks. 'That was quick" said the sister,' they must have heard about you Dad and weren't fancying another battle!' The Golden harp fairly lighting up his face, the Faither read aloud the wording in the passport Irish Passport, dated 25th September 2002:-

'Name - McGinley, Neil; Date of Birth - 04/12/1918; Nationality - Eireannach, 'I think that's the pronunciation all right, it means Irish in Irish. Irish in brackets it says; Place of Birth - Dun Na Ngall with Donegal in brackets, they sound the same in Irish and English if you say them quick aye - Dun Na Ngall - Donegal.' The Faither gave a wee smile, his eyes lighting up. With his wee polished face shining, his heart was bursting with the pride with joy of it, the twins were delighted for him and so were all the brothers when they heard the news.

'We've got a wee surprise Dad' said the sister who by this time had been joined by her Twin. 'We were thinking Dad, that after all the bother that you went to getting the passport you will need to christen it! What with the boys back and forward to Ireland, although I think that was a bonus for them. Francie and Peggy Mickie Owen, Anthony and Brid Dora, all signing the documents and swearing that they knew you. Aye and Owenie, and Brid, and Brid's brother Michael signing it as commissioner. 'Aye and Father Pat Ward at Kincasslagh was a great help' offered the other sister. 'Aye everyone was great' agreed the Faither, 'but I've never heard of a passport, Irish or not, being baptized' The sisters laughed and explained what they were meaning was that the Faither was to pick anywhere in the whole world he would like to visit and off the three of them would go and they would get the passport stamped!. 'Anywhere in the world you want to go to Dad' said the Sisters in unison. 'We'll give you a few days to think it over and we'll get booked up.' The girls offered a few suggestions to get the Faither

thinking. 'What about South Africa where you and mum once had a wee inclination to emigrate to ? Or maybe Malaya or Malaysia as its now called?' We've heard you singing Moonlight Oe'r Malaya a few times Dad, what about a wee trip to Malaya and we could take in Thailand where you were a POW? Maybe you like a wee visit there almost 60 years after your captivity .' The Sisters had made this journey a few years previously and had visited the grave of the Faither's best pal Duncan McShane who had perished in the camps. Anywhere you fancy Dad. We'll leave you to think about it.'
Next morning after breakfast the Faither announced that after a lot of thinking he had plumped for a trip to Rome.!! - "Faith of our Faither's" right enough! Rome it was. The girls swiftly swept into action and the air tickets and accommodation were booked and within a fortnight the Faither and the sisters were on their way to the Vatican. This would be the Faither's second visit to Rome.

In June 1975, the Faither, Mum, the twins and the youngest brother who wisnae spoiled, drove from Kirkmichael in Helensburgh to Rome and back again. McGinleys on Tour, pulling a Sprite caravan. The trip took them through parts of Belgium, France, Austria, Germany, over the Swiss Alps (Yodeledeeeteee) and down through Italy to Rome. The sister drove all the way with the Faither as the navigator. The Faither would study the map in great detail and advise at intervals, where the next turn off would be. The Sister had already worked this all out but the Faither would insist in navigating. The Faither liked the maps. When he heard of the intended journey and that the mode of travel was car and caravan and that Faither was the navigator, Father John McCabe gave the twins a Miraculous Medal of Our Lady prior to setting out on their journey. 'I think, he thought, it would be a miracle if we got there and back home in the one piece !!' suggested the sisters.

Three weeks later: 'Turn left at the top of Henry Bell Street and we are Home!'

The trip was a great success as the Faither navigated them from Kirkmichael to Rome and back. The brothers who had been left at home had great parties listening to Tubular Bells in the absence of their touring parents and siblings. There was one major hiccup up on that Rome trip. (the Granda who was from Donegal had a great cure for hiccups. He used to say in his soft Donegal voice, if you said Welcome stranger, welcome stranger, with your eyes shut and kept repeating these words then your hiccups would go away and it worked).

'Look at the window in our car' said the Sister. 'Somebody has spammed in the window! The glove compartment has been forced open. Oh Naw! The passports are missing!' screeched the sister. I think there would a few wee sweary words being confessed to when the Sister next went to confession. The Faither travelled on a UK Visitors Passports in those days, then available from post offices without proof of birth.

Nae passports. I don't think that this wee hiccup would go away with a few wee welcome strangers. A long day of frustrating questions and red tape at the British Consulate but as quick as you can say 'welcome stranger' the problem was solved and soon forgotten.

An excited Faither, dressed in checked shirt, Donegal Tweed jacket, which he had bought in Magees in Donegal Town a few years previously and decked with Donegal tweed bunnet (a bit to the side) was ready for the airport and his next visit to Rome. Nae Sprite caravan this time - they were going to spoil the Faither and do Rome in style, so the flights and a 5 star hotel was booked. ' You've the hotel already booked, that's good we'll no have any bother looking for somewhere to stay when we get to Rome .' observed the Faither. The girls smiled.

The Faither got his passport stamped and christened at Roma airport and together with the sisters had four wonderful days. The faither would fit in anywhere and was quite at home with the five star treatment. On first full day they decided to go to Saint Peter's and on arrival saw that Mass was about to start. The sisters told us that what they witnessed was as unbelievable as it was unexpected (I think that wee Miraculous Medal from the first Rome trip was still at work!!) As they sat in a half empty basilica, taking in the surroundings, there was a trumpet blast and down the aisle was a grand troupe of cardinals followed by, being carried aloft, and the Holy Father Pope John Paul ll. The Mass the sisters learned was being offered for all bishops of the Church who had died in the previous year. The Pope, from his chair delivered the homily and at the end of Mass, as the cardinals paraded back up the aisle, the Pope within touching distance of the Faither looked at him and blessed him, with Faither holding aloft holy medals and rosaries purchased in the Vatican shop earlier that morning. So the rosaries which the Faither and the sisters handed out to the family on their return home had truly been blessed by the Pope. 'Nane of yer holding up the rosary beads in vast crowd in St Peter's Square towards a wee white dot in the distance.'

During the next four days Faither and the girls toured the Vatican, the Sistine Chapel, Saint Paul Outside the Walls, the Forum, the Colosseum, the Spanish Steps, Ancient Rome with a Roman guide...it was all great! Then they traveled a few hours by train and had a brilliant three days in Venice with Faither going up and down every canal in Venice (just wan cornetto!), hopping on and off the vaparetto river buses and being hugely interested in the decaying buildings on the water (a wee bit rising damp there!) and architectural beauty of Saint Mark's Square and the ancient buildings of this amazing city. A great holiday to christen the passport, but oh what was to follow on his future trips was truly a hail, hail glorious 2003 for the Faither with his newly acquired Irish Passport being kept busy!

In September 2002 Celtic were knocked out of the European Champions Qualifiers and were parachuted into the UEFA Cup and what a run they had in this competition. The Faither made full use of his Irish Passport and along with his McGinley bhoys, big Willie & John Wilson he travelled round Europe supporting the Celts all the way to Seville when the sisters took Faither to the UEFA Cup Final, accompanied by the oldest and the youngest brothers and nephews Paul, Kevin and Tom....The McGinley Eightsome Reel in Seville!! They were all On the One Road!

Unfortunately, Porto defeated the Celts....but 'what the hell do we care now' as wee Jock and Todd would sing and everyone in Seville had a grand old time supporting a grand old team and what the hell did they care.....a once in a lifetime brilliant experience for all the McGinleys and the other 70,000 who traveled to Sevilla.....officially honoured by UEFA in 2003 as the best supporters in Europe!!

The fairytale to the Final started with Celtic beating minnows FK Suduka 10-1 on aggregate, followed by beating Blackburn Rovers home and away. Faither loved the one nil victory at Parkhead in October 2002 and gave his away tickets to grandsons Paul and Neil who greatly enjoyed the experience as Celtic romped to a two nil victory down at Blackburn. It was payback time to Graeme Souness for his arrogance at Celtic Park when he had compared Blackburn to Celtic as men against boys! 'Men against Boys? Aye well the Bhoys sure shut him up good and proper! Aye it put his gas on a peep!' the Faither concluded.

In the next round the following month Faither traveled to Spain with the eldest brother, Willie and John Wilson where they watched Celtic being beaten 2-1 by Celta Vigo, a celebration night nonetheless as Celtic went through on the away goals rule, having won 1-0 in the home tie. By all accounts it was a Hail Hail Viva Espana trip as the Celta Vigo supporters were so welcoming and friendly.

The next adventure and the next stamp on the Faither's passport was a German stamp . Celtic had beaten crack German side VfB Stuggart 3-1 in a tremendous match at Parkhead and the Faither had been in a hail hail happy mood for the next week, looking forward to being a Tim on Tour in Germany. And so it came to pass that in February 2003 that the youngest brother, accompanied the Faither to Stuggart along with Willie and John Wilson. Celtic were beaten 3-2 on the night but yet again it was a glorious European night for the Celts who were marching into the next round against the mighty Liverpool. A bit of a celebration ensued. Faither bumped into our pal Paul Friel at the game and hugs and travel tales were exchanged. The craic was mighty! Back at the hotel, The brother left the Faither in the company of the Wilsons and went for a pub crawl. ' I like to look about places that are new to me and see the culture so I 'm going out for a wee dander' said the fireman. ' You'll be fine here wae Big Willie. Eh Dad?' 'Aye nae bother son, I'll just sit and have a wee Guinness and maybe another wee half and I'll be heading for bed. Don't be getting lost and no too much culture now' grinned the Faither as the brother headed for the hot spots of Stuggart.' 'Don't mention the War now!'

The brother, on returning to the hotel, in the early hours of the following morning tiptoed into the room which he was sharing with the Faither. He got the fright of his life. Shock! Horror! Then panic set in, sobering him up quickly. Faither's bed was empty. The Faither wasn't in his room. 'Oh my God!' What am I gonnae do? The twins will kill me!!' The last thing the girls had said to the brother before departing from Rhu was ' Mind and keep an eye on Dad all the time and don't leave him for a minute. OK!' 'Oh My God! The brother nipped along the corridor and knocked Big Willie's room door.

Is ma Dad in there Willie? Have you seen my dad?' 'Are you at the kidding?....he was with you when I went to bed' said Willie who was an early-bedder. It was you who was in charge and looking after him!' The brother was white with fear.' I was sure Faither would be safe enough in the hotel wae the Wilsons!'' Hail Mary full of grace....' "Nothing else for it but to go to reception and ask them to contact the polis and report a missing 84 year old man". So down the stairs the brother went hoping that the receptionist and the Gestapo spoke English ' Don't mention the war...good advice 'the brother was thinking. As the brother was passing the resident's lounge on the way he heard a familiar song being sung. "It's 4 o'clock in the morning! Am I imagining this?' thought the brother. There in the corner sitting back in an armchair was the Faither, sitting wae a group of stalwarts, singing The Fields Of Athenry, with a row of empty glasses and some full ones in front of him. What a man and what a constitution. The Faither was loving it!! 'Did you find any culture son?' The brother, well he was greatly relieved but got belters when he got home for not looking after the Faither!! What a night and what an experience. The ould passport was being put to good use all right! Celtic now into the quarter-final of the UEFA Cup, and about to take on favourites Liverpool.

March 2003 and once again Neilly was in his beloved Paradise and the twins and the brother that's going to Mullaghduff for the match against Liverpool. It was a cracking game ending one apiece. The supporters of both sides belted out 'Walk On' with gusto and Celtic Park rocked with the atmosphere and although the

Hoops still sung Walk On With Hope In Your Heart, few believed they would overcome Liverpool at Annfield....although the Faither did and let the dissenters know it!. Faither always looked on the bright side of life! A month later the Celtic support travelled to Liverpool in their thousands and once again dad gave his two tickets to grandsons Paul and Neil to enjoy the European experience. The Faither would watch the game on the giant telly that the sisters bought when the Faither's sight was failing. The Sisters would watch the game with him and have the pies heated in the oven for half time. The Faither in gifting the tickets for Liverpool to the grateful grandsons said' sure I'll wait until the passport is needed again and you don't need a passport for England! Oh What A night. Celtic beat the favourites Liverpool 2-0 at Annfield. Ferry Coach House, Rhu was jumping and rocked to' You'll never Walk Alone!' Celtic were going to Portugal for the semi-final to play Boavista and the Faither was angling to go.

In April 2003, Faither along with three of the brothers watched Celtic draw one each with Boavista at Parkhead and once again the Celtic legions thought this may be the end of the European adventure, but not our dad...he was looking forward to getting a Portugese stamp on his passport and he thought Celtic were going to win...and he was right because he went, he had a great time and Celtic beat Boavista 1-0.

Now it was onto Seville for the Final and the Faither was going back to Spain again to see the Celts!
There was one wee problem however, another wee hiccup! 'Welcome Stranger! Welcome Stranger!'

The sister who organises the travel arrangements like Mammy was a wee bit superstitious. Nae new shoes on the table! Nae cutting your nails on a Sunday. Nae umbrellas up in the house! Never bet on Celtic or Rangers! Mammy was superstitious about wearing green but the sisters hadn't adopted that one and were bedecked in emerald green in Seville. The superstitious sister would not tempt fate by booking for Seville before Celtic got to the Final. When she tried and tried, and tried, all flights to Seville were booked...what we gonnae do she said to the twin who could speak a bit of Spanish as a result of her two years voluntary work in Panama 20 years earlier. 'I'll try in Spanish but it's been twenty years' she replied and she did Parliama Espana all over the place, and succeeded. Flights were booked Glasgow to London to Bilbao to Sevilla. Bit of a long route to take but Oh We're Going To Sevilla sang the twins....and dad was going to Spain again....and the oldest brother and his son Tom. After phoning half the hotels in Seville, Mary got rooms booked in the Alcazar Hotel and as it turned out, this was round the corner from Celtic's official meeting point for supporters and the McGinley party had a great pre-match night singing along to Charlie And The Bhoys. (Charlie has since moved to Mullaghduff). Big Willie and John were not traveling with Faither, they choosing instead to travel via Portugal, where Willie had a beautiful villa, visited by mum, dad and the twins some years earlier. They missed a great party.

On 21st May 2003, the 84 year old Faither was in his glory, sitting high in the grandstand in sunny Seville watching his beloved Celtic in a European Final, with his twin daughters and nephew Kevin by his side, all singing along with the sea of green and white all around the stadium. The Rhu party had walked up 'the Green Mile' where the green and white hoops of Celtic stretched back as far as the eye could see. They bumped into family friend Terence Friel who was a lost bhoy who had lost his way to his supporters club bus. Walk On Terence said the faither and you'll find it! Anthony Peggy Boyle and his son Lee from Mullaghduff were in the same area of the stand! Did Grace let you off the hook for a few days.' quipped the Faither. 'Aye the gang's all here! Neilly !'

It didn't matter that Celtic were beaten in extra-time in that epic Final - it was a privilege and a joy for the eight McGinleys to be there in all four corners of the stadium. It was singalong partytime for the next two days in Seville . It was like a stuck record with the whole repertoire of Celtic favourites being sung over and over again. It was brill! 'Hail! Hail! The Celts are Here' was repeated several times by the Faither whose voice was starting to croak a wee bit. The Fields of Athenry got big licks and were well watered. ' We're on the One Road' which we would always sing on the way to catch the ferry at Stranraer got an airing in Seville as well. The last day was spent taking in the great sights of Seville, praying and lighting a candle for mammy in the cathedral; and having a beer on the steps of the cathedral along with a multitude of Celtic fans all singing' We Don't Care If We Win, Lose, or Draw. What the Hell do we care now .. For its…'

The passport was used by the Faither many more times as he flew from Prestwick to the strand at Carrickfinn to visit his homeland – after 9/11 a passport was needed to fly to Donegal. Aye, the Faither, our Dad, had great joy and happy times with his Irish Passport.

'When Faither got his Irish passport
His heart was filled with joy
The pride was burstin oot o' him
Like a wean wae a new toy
The bother Faither went to was worth it
The hastles and forms to fill
It took him to Rome to see the Pope
And the Celts in Germany, Spain and Portugal, then Seville!'

Almost three years after Neilly got his Irish passport his cousin Brid Dora McGinley from Annagry discovered, while church records were being computerized that Neilly had in fact been baptized at St Mary Star of the Sea Church at Annagry, and not at St Mary's in Kinncasslagh! Brid obtained a copy of the Birth and Baptismal certificates duly signed by Father Michael Herrity at Annagry, and posted this on to Neilly in Rhu. What a laugh everyone had!

Neil (with a little help from the twins)

Losing Terence

Time passed and Neilly spent many of his twilight years contentedly tending the large country garden of the Coach house in Rhu. Nothing life had thrown at him, had changed his beautiful heart, and he was always there to support, and comfort, family, friend, or stranger who needed his help. In May 2001 my mother Neilly's youngest sister Patsy, lost her first son Terence. She and my Father Ross were utterly devastated. Indeed the loss of the first son was to have a profound effect on my father's mental health. With the help of all the family, in particular Neilly and the twins Kathleen and Mary, my Mother some how managed to carry on. Her heart was broken, and still is, yet she lives with this.

For me the day I lost my brother was one of the very worst I have ever experienced. At the time I was running my own little children's nursery in the village of Barcaldine a few minutes drive from Benderloch where I still live today. The nursery was closed on that day, as it was the funeral of the best friend I will ever have. Jean and I had known one another since I was in my mid twenties, when I moved from Dunbeg just outside the town of Oban to the village of Benderloch. Jean and her husband Hugh McColl owned all the land which had formerly been Keil farm. As the farm was no longer in existence Hugh and Jean were selling a few plots of their land for house building. We were lucky enough to be able to purchase about a quarter of an acre on the lower slopes of Ben Lora. On this beautiful spot we built the house we still have today. Jean and I became close friends, and when I began my children's nursery Jean who also loved children became a very valued and much loved member of staff at the centre. Tragically Jean was to lose her life to lung cancer.

The funeral was held in the little local church in Benderloch. St Modans was crammed full of folk, who wanted to say good bye to an incredible lady. The service was so very moving, and I was unable to stop the tears from flowing. Outside the church when the ceremony was over, unable to face the burial of my best friend at Achnnaba cemetery, instead I invited the two members of nursery staff Mary and Karen, who were with me, back to my house for coffee. Together we walked up the track from the church to my home. When we reached the steep drive leading to the house, I was puzzled, my husband Ian and my son Mark, both of whom should have been at work, at this time of the day, were sitting out on the balcony at the front of the house. Although I asked them why they were there neither spoke. Mary Karen and I climbed the front steps and entered the house.

Showing the ladies into the living room I then went into the kitchen to put the kettle on to boil. Ian and Mark were somehow already there before me, and both looked extremely distressed. Before I could ask why, Ian stepped towards me, and with tears spilling from his eyes, blurted out "Your Dad phoned.

Terence died this morning!" This short sudden news was like a vicious blow to my heart and my head simultaneously. All I could do was to cry out "No, No, No." Hearing my cries Mary came running through to the kitchen. "What is it Liz, are you still upset about Jean?" I don't remember what I replied or whether any of us did get tea or coffee that day, only that after talking to my mother and father on the phone, I sat late into the night, and remembered my brother.

Less than two years separated us in age, and when we were both small children we were in fact inseparable. When he was still a baby in his pram I lavished him with hugs and kisses. Confusingly for me, as a baby he did not return my affections. One time when I leaned into his pram and tried to cuddle him, his chubby baby fingers grasped a chunk of my baby fine hair, and ripped it out of my head by the roots. I squealed and cried in true pain. "Don't make such a fuss" my Mother scolded, "he is only a baby, and he didn't really mean to hurt you. My Mother was right, as throughout our childhood and beyond my little brother Terence was devoted to me. However when he was still a babe in pram, and despite my hair injury, I was impatient to make him love me.

One sunny day I watched my Mother wheel Terence in his pram outside, and leave him asleep in the garden. "Can I take my baby brother for a walk in his pram please?" I pleaded with my Mother. "No, you're much too small to take him" she replied. "Just play in the garden, and keep an eye on your baby brother, while I get on with the washing" Then turning around she walked back up the path, opened the front door, and disappeared into the little house.

Seconds later, I made my move. Releasing the pram brake, and opening the garden gate I pushed my little brother out of the garden through the grounds of the wood yard, and on to the pavement by the main road. I had no real plan of where I might go. I was just determined to have my baby brother all to myself for a little while. I had only travelled about half a street length, when I heard my Mother frantically calling to me. I'm not sure if it was fear of my Mother's fury or just plain stubbornness that made me start to run with my brother in the pram. It was just as well the streets were quiet, as while I was running with the pram I was too small to see over the hood to see where I was going.

Soon I reached a busier part of town. With my Mother's screams still ringing in my ears, I pushed my brother's pram across the very busy Sinclair St. Sinclair St is an extremely steep road which sweeps down through the centre of the town to the esplanade and sea front. Having crossed to the other side of the road, I began to push the pram down hill. The steepness of the street caused the vehicle to gather speed. Faster and faster it rushed, barely missing startled pedestrians. I was now terrified and clung desperately to the pram handle hopelessly trying to slow the now out of control buggy. Thankfully my Mother's screams of panic, alerted a young policeman's attention, and coming out of the police station saw the pram hurtling towards him. He dashed out into the path of the run away vehicle and acting as a human bumper managed to bring it to a halt. His quick reactions undoubtedly prevented a serious accident, for if unstopped the pram my brother and I were heading for the busy traffic light cross roads where Princes St cuts through Sinclair St.

My only memories of the return walk were of my traumatised Mother pushing baby Terence in the pram with one hand, and hauling me far too tightly by the other, and somehow also managing to slap my legs, frequently on the journey. I also remember meeting Neilly with his young son Johnnie on the way home. I was very glad of that for he was able to calm my Mother, and the hot stinging smacks to my little skinny legs, slowly subsided. The shock of this whole incident did not change my behaviour for very long. As Terence progressed to a toddler he was my constant companion, and all day long we would play together in the grounds of the wood yard. Yet soon I was up to my old tricks again.

One particularly warm sunny summer's day I asked my mother if she would take us down to the beach. My Mother said she was much to busy, and told us just to play in the sandpit in the garden. As soon as my Mother was inside the house, and safely out of sight, I took Terence's chubby little hand, and led him out of the garden. The beach was only about 15 minutes walk away. Mother had often taken us there, and I knew the way well.

When we arrived at the esplanade still holding hands we made our way to the area were the beach ponies worked beside the pier. The beach was crowded with families with children, all enjoying the sand and sunshine.

Terence and I stood for a while watching all the other children being lifted on to the beach ponies for rides along the sands. We both desperately wanted to be one of these lucky children being hoisted on to the beach ponies. However we had no money to pay for a ride. "Why you're such cute little kids" sounded a voice above me. "What are your names?" All kids are cute, but I suppose my little brother and I were especially cute. I spent a great deal of time outdoors, and my skin was a cool pale brown. This with my light blonde hair and pale green grey eyes probably made me an attractive if skinny young child. Cutest by far was my little Terence. Soft and chubby with a mass of golden red curly hair, and skin covered in golden freckles. I looked up to find to find the owner of the soft Yankee drawl. Towering above me was a smiling faced young American sailor in his smart navy uniform and white pork pie sailor's hat I told him our names, though I don't remember his. He asked us where our folks were. I pointed in the direction we had just come. I am sure he must have thought that our "folks" were just further along the beach. The amiable young man then swooped up my little brother and placed him on a large piebald pony named Big Fella. For a moment I thought that I was going to be left behind. Not so, as the charming

young sailor also swung me up and planted me securely behind my brother on the large pony.
The young man then walked beside us as the youngster in charge of the gentle Big Fella , led the animal along the beach ride route.

Young children live only for the moment, and as the warm and comfortable animal trudged and swayed along the sand I was never happier. I wrapped my arms around my little brother to make him feel safe, and all my small senses breathed in the wonders of the day. The steady stride of the patient pony, as it's hoofs crunched through the gravely sand, the soft warm breeze which carried the salty smell of the sea, the happy sounds of laughter of the people on the beach, and the re-assuring warmth of that then more gentle sun was perfect happiness to me. When I was just a few years older, about eight of age, I did spend all my summer school holidays working with the beach ponies on that same beach, with the same patient, and gentle animals.

After the ride the kind hearted young sailor bought my brother and I, extra large deliciously cold ice cream cones, which we quickly devoured. By now the kind sailor had begun to realise that the two cute little people he had befriended were not with a parent, but had some how managed to slip out of their home, and come to the beach without their parent's knowledge. He asked me if I knew my way home. I said of course I did, and I would get my little brother safely home. However the caring young man decided to accompany us. Terence was now getting tired.

His short toddler legs were not able to walk very far. "Lillabet Lillabet carry me" he whinged to me.
The kind stranger lifted him on to his high shoulders, and followed me the few streets home.

My poor mother must have been frantic with fear and worry, when she discovered we were missing. Yet I was completely unconcerned and entirely oblivious of the pain I had caused her. As we passed through the archway and into the wood yard our friendly sailor became confused. "Little Lizzie are you sure you know where you are going?" he gently inquired. "Yes it's just a wee bit further" I confidently replied. When we finally arrived at our front gate, a large group was gathered in front of the cottage. I could see my mum and dad, who must have come home from work in the middle of the day, as had my Uncle Neilly who was also there. A number of our neighbours and a policeman were among the group. My Mother read the situation at once, and running towards me took my arm and dragged me through the garden gate. Then propelled me, through the front door of the house. "You little rascal!" she screamed. Thankfully my hero Neilly quickly followed us into the house. "Don't be too hard on her Patsy, she's just a little adventurer" he pleaded.

Super baby Tommy

Later when my Mother's anger cooled and she decided that she could now trust me more she allowed us to go to the local corner shop for odd errands. It was there that we met Charlie the cobbler. Charlie's workshop was housed in the same building as the corner shop and Charlie was not just an ordinary shoe mender, he was a story teller, who knew perfectly how to entertain and capture the imagination of little children. We had very recently had an addition to our family baby Thomas was only a few weeks old. Thomas or Tommy as he was called by all of us was a cross and fractious baby, he slept little and when awake cried incessantly. In our cramped conditions in the forgotten but and ben cottage, life was difficult for Terence and I and also for my Mum and Dad. Five of us all trying to sleep in one tiny bedroom. My Mum and Dad were exhausted. My little brother and I were completely fed up with this new little intruder. The very wise Charlie the cobbler knew this, and while he was mending folk's shoes, sitting with a shoe on the laste, he would frequently remove the tacks from his mouth, to tell us the most fantastic tales about Super baby Tommy.

Baby Tommy was not just a crabby wee Infant, not at all. After midnight when the rest of the family were eventually sleeping Super baby Tommy would climb out of his cot, tiptoe out of the front door, and then soar high into the night sky. This little figure in his white baby grow looping diving, and flying through the night air looking for some mischief he could enjoy, while the rest of the town was asleep. Indeed he was a very very mischievous baby, who caused havoc in the night and played endless tricks on the inhabitants of Helensburgh. As Charlie spun his tales, tapped and mended the shoes, Terence and I hung on his every word enthralled by each story he told. The stories were often very funny, and my brother and I would collapse giggling on the cobbler's wooden floor, gasping for breath, and begging for more.

The accident

On that awful day when I knew Terence had died I thought of Terence, and those innocent childhood days, and wished we were all children again. My only regret that will be forever with me is my own inability to say that I loved him. I thought without words he always knew that I did. Yet actions were not enough for him, and when we were a few years older Terence needed the words, indeed one time pleaded for those words. I had just had a nearly very serious accident in the grand and beautiful Hermitage Park in my home town of Helensburgh.

One sunny summer Sunday when many families were enjoying pleasant picnics on the neat green grass, of the well kept park, a gang of young children were enjoying more challenging pursuits. The group of friends, cousins and brothers, not content to sit in the sun, were climbing trees in the park. Some of these trees were perched on a very steep bank overlooking a small stream which flowed through the park. My brother Terence and I foolishly decided to tackle a tall and slender young ash tree, which was already slanted at a precarious angle over the stream bank.

Being a little older slimmer and more agile I soon scrambled higher up the tree than my brother. Near the top of the tree I began to feel the effort of the climb. The day was hot and my hands were warm and sticky. One hand lost the grip on a fairly strong and secure branch. The danger of my situation now hit me, and I tried to grab on to another tree branch to secure my position and prevent me from falling. It was all too quick and the branch I had managed to grasp sheered from the tree. I then crashed through all the lower branches of the ash tree landing on my back, tree branch still in my hand, on the small rocks and stones of the shallow stream. For a few seconds I lay there slightly stunned and afraid to move.

As I was lying in the stream, I could see my little brother had come down from that tree and was now standing on the lower part of the burn bank, both palms of his small hands together, arms outstretched, as if were preparing to make the classic comic book dive, at the same time calling out "Lillabet Lillabet I will save you. I love you. I love you." Instead of appreciating the bravery and devotion of this darling seven year old sibling, all I could think was, that the water in which I was lying was barely 3 inches deep, and how ridiculous that my silly little brother, could possibly think that he could dive in and save me? However aware that Terence was a clumsy little kid, and afraid that he would actually attempt my rescue and fall on his head, I staggered to my feet and lifted him down from the bank. Hand in hand we wadded to the other side of the burn, scrambled out, and walked over the little bridge.

Nearby some friends of my parents were enjoying their Sunday picnic on the grass. Terence ran to them, still worried that I might be hurt, told the folk what had happened. After much fussing and back rubbing I realised that there was no pain from my accident not a single tiny twinge. The whole incident had upset my brother much more than me. Never the less I did not feel like eating the food that was offered, at the time, and instead left Terence in the care of the family, and made my way out of the park to my Grandparent's home.

When I arrived at my Grandparent's house they were just about to start their Sunday meal. I dearly loved both my Grandparents but was always slightly in awe of my grandfather. When I was younger Granddad would take me for long walks while my Mother was attending Sunday Mass. He would buy me little treats of chocolate and sweets, and I would chatter constantly to him. However he was a man of few words, and spoke only rarely to me. Once on our walks we arrived at the pier in Helens burgh. My small legs were tired and I sat down to rest on one of the metal capstans boats used to tie up on. "Don't sit on that cold thing!" my Granddad said sharply. "You'll get piles!" "What's piles Granddad?" I asked. My Grandfather did not reply, only turned his head away and looked out to sea. I did not ask him again, but I never sat on anything cold again in fear of contracting some horrible disease. My Grandfather fetched another chair, and my Grandmother ladled out the first course of their meal. No sooner than I had taken a few spoonfuls of the potato and leek soup than I felt quite ill, and leaving the table, went into the bathroom and was sick.

Later that night when were settled down in our beds. Terence seemed unable to sleep, and kept talking about the events of the day. I was grumpy and tired and told him to be quiet. "But I thought you might be dead when you were lying there so still in the river, and I could not bear that. I love you so much." Then in a little pleading voice asked "Do you love me like I love you?" By this time my patience was wearing very thin, and more sharply I told my brother to be quiet, as he would waken my youngest brother Tommy who was sleeping in his cot. Terence did not speak again, but I remember him still, crying softly in the night. Even now I feel mean and cruel that I was too stubborn and selfish to say the words he needed to hear.

However growing up we remained close. During his very rocky marriage of seven years I tried to be the peace maker in the hope that he and his wife might resolve their problems. When his marriage failed I spent time trying to comfort and support my brother. One of the problems was the lack of any children, and when he finally met his last partner Margaret they decided to try I.V.F treatment. After two failed attempts Margaret became pregnant with triplets. The couple were ecstatic. Sadly the pregnancy was only to last four months. Then Margaret went into premature labour and lost all three babies. Six weeks later on the morning of my friend Jean's funeral, Terence died of a massive heart attack.

Saying Goodbye

The shock of Terence's sudden death affected us all badly. My parents were grief stricken and relied heavily on my youngest brother Tommy for support at this dreadful time. As always Neilly was there for my Mother, and also for my Father. On the Day of the funeral with his arm around my Mother, he rode in the car with my Father, Margaret and I. I was so glad he was with us as I was afraid the pain of Terence's last journey would be too much for her my Mother. All the slow journey to the graveyard Neilly held his youngest sister's hand and spoke quietly to her. He talked of his Son Owen and his wife Rita, both of whom had already passed away. What he said was not gloomy or sad. Instead he spoke in a light hearted way about the funny moments and happy memories he had of them both. I think now that he was trying to occupy my Mother's mind, and help keep her spirits composed enough to face the sad task ahead.

The day was warm and the sun shone that day at the graveyard. After the service was over one of the twins spoke to my Mother and I. Pointing at her Mother Rita's gravestone Mary joked "Sure Terence will be fine here just a little way from Mammy. She will keep an eye on him." "Aye" said the other twin Kathleen. "Mammy will make sure he doesn't climb over the wall and go for a few too many drinks in the County bar. Well at least not too often."

Not long after Terence's death in May 2001 my Mother's sister Sadie was diagnosed with terminal lung cancer. Aunt Sadie had moved into my Grandmother's house after losing her husband Paddy at a young age. She was a much loved sister and aunt, and was always on hand to help the rest of the family whenever needed. The news was devastating for her and the family. Ill and weakened by courses of radiotherapy, on her discharge from the Western Infirmary, Sadie came to stay with my mum and dad, and was lovingly cared for at 13 Charlotte St until her death six months later. Perhaps in caring for Sadie my parents were for this time able to focus on Sadie, and not their grief for the loss of their son.

However the shock of my brother's sudden death affected my parents deeply, and looking back I feel that was the beginning of my Father's confusion, and memory loss. At first it was just the small things, which were almost funny, if they had not been a sober warning of yet worse times to come. The time he decided to cut the grass, with the carpet Hoover instead of the grass mower.

My Mother rushed after him before any of the neighbours could see his mistake. Even as years passed my Father would often forget that Terence was no longer with us, and ask my Mother in his agitated way, why his son had not called in to see them. My poor Mother repeatedly had to patiently explain the sad truth which caused them both to relive the grief of their loss. As a result of his worsening diabetes and transient strokes my Father became more confused and frail.

Eventually Mother stopped trying to explain, and would simply say that Terence was just busy pruning the roses in his garden. My Father seemed happy with that reply to his question. That to is how I like to think of my brother now, for I no longer believe in the heaven I was told about as a child. For me Terence will be forever in that garden tending his beloved roses, and by his side, looking so much like him so long ago, a chubby little child, with masses of pale red hair and skin covered in golden freckles. Close by are three little dark haired girls, dressed in more modern outfits, squealing in delight as they play in the garden, happy as sunshine and free as the wind, the little triplets that he and Margaret almost had.

Despite all the trials in his life Neilly's strong spirit was still with him, and although his health was not as robust as it had been, he still did his very best to support all his family, through any difficult times, at the same time finding the strength to help my Mum and Dad. He and the twins Kathleen and Mary were constant in my parent's life, as was my youngest brother Tommy and his family.

Getting older

My Father's health was deteriorating rapidly, and now the twins spent many hours transporting him and my mum to endless clinics, and hospital appointments. Neilly had to spend these hours alone at the coach house in Rhu. Sadly Dad's health continued to worsen and he lost his mobility. He was confined to a wheel chair, and could only walk short distances with the aid of a zimmer frame. Mum was remarkable in the way she looked after him. Support was provided by local nursing services. However Mum had most of the work done before they arrived. My brother Tommy would look in every day, and on Sundays would get dad well wrapped up, and take him out in the wheel chair. Dad always looked forward to this weekly outing. Mum was able to listen to Mass on the Irish radio station while the men were out.

Sadly Neilly's sight was now failing. The condition was not curable. Neilly made no fuss, just stoically carried on as best he could. Still able to find his way around the house and go for quiet country walks through the small village of Rhu. One day when the twins had had to spend almost a full day with my parents at a hospital in Glasgow they returned home to find their Father still sitting in the now dark conservatory, where they had left him early that morning. He had dozed off on throughout the day, and did not seem to be able to see that it was now dark.

"How were Patsy and Ross?" were his first words to his daughters.

One of the last memories of my Uncle was at my Mum and Dad's 60th Wedding Anniversary. The event was organised by my brother Tommy and his wife Ann Marie, and held at their home at Colgrain in Helensburgh. A home celebration was thought more suitable than a meal out, as my Dad was now very frail, and he was apt to doze off frequently throughout the day. My son Mark and my youngest daughter Sarah Anne were with us. However my older daughter Kirstin was unable to make the five hour car journey from her family home in Nairn. Kirstin had suffered from a painful back condition since the death of her little two and a half year old son Callum John. Callum had been born with a severe brain condition which meant that he was both blind and deaf, had little control of his muscles, and needed oxygen to help him breath. Nevertheless Kirstin and her husband Andrew were devoted to their small son, and had cared for him with endless patience and love. Although an operation on her spine had greatly improved her condition, a recent incident during work had damaged her back again.

My Brother Tommy's girls were wonderful Julie Clare and Bernadette spent most of the day handing out glasses of champagne and dishing out delicious food from the beautiful buffet they and their Mum had prepared. Tommy's big son Anthony was also very helpful on the day. Little Monica so beautifully behaved, helped her mum Julie serve food to all the Family.

The twins Kathleen and Mary had brought Neilly to the party. At one point in the day the conversation turned to the paintings on my Brother's living room wall, most of which were mine. My brother still harbours a lost hope, that one day my art work might become valuable. Over the years I have gifted, and he has bought some of my art efforts. Neilly by now almost totally blind interjected. "I've still got the best painting in the world". Meaning the painting of his parents in Mullaghduff in Donegal Ireland, which I had painted for his birthday some years before. There was a little stab in my heart, as I realised that he could no longer see the picture that he loved so much. Yet as if he could read my mind Neilly then said "Don't worry I can still see it very clearly in my minds eye."

Peaceful Passing

Just less than a year later Neilly was sitting in his chair in the bedroom of his home at Rhu having a cup of tea with the twins, when he felt very unwell. The twins helped their father to his bed. A few minutes later Neilly closed his eyes and quietly slipped away.

Neilly's funeral was huge. Every seat in St Joseph's church was filled, and crowds were crushed in to the grounds out side the church. It seemed like half the town was there to salute my Uncle's passing. The service was unbelievably moving. The mass and homily were carried out beautifully by Father Paul Friel a dear family friend.

Afterwards a long throng of mourners followed the funeral car on foot the last long mile to the graveyard. Neilly was laid to rest beside his beloved Rita, and near his son Owen. I thought then that it truly had been a privilege to have known such a wonderful man. Although sad at his passing, still I was happy that none of life's trials had managed to change his brave spirit.

When Neilly died he was less than two months short of his eighty ninth birthday. I believe Neilly knew that his life was closing, and I am sure he often thought of the loved ones who had gone before him, his beloved wife Rita, his handsome son Owen, his baby twin boys, his brave hearted friend Owenie Burke, who had saved his life, when he was a young man toiling on death railway. I am also sure Neilly thought also of Duncan his childhood friend. The friend he had grown up with, and loved so much. The friend he had to helplessly watch die from dysentery in that camp from hell all those years ago powerless to help him.

I thought that a fitting conclusion to my Uncle's book might be a final verse to Neilly's poem which I found as a child in that leather bound book, in my Grandmother's old sideboard drawer.

Without his permission yet I hope his approval, I have written the final verse of Neilly's poem.

Duncan my friend, I know now my own life is coming to an end,
For me it has been the most wonderful life, and always on the way,
I have tried to live it as best I could for both of us,
I only hope, that you may now feel, that I have done it well.

Lost Souls

The graves of the men who died while building and maintaining the Burma Thailand railway, who were mainly buried by the sides of the railway they constructed were transferred to three war cemeteries. Those recovered from the southern part of the line were re-interred in the Chungkai and Kanchanaburi War Cemeteries in Thailand. Those who lost their lives at the northern part of the line were re-interred in the war cemetery at Thanbyuzayat. Others who have no known graves are commemorated on memorials in other areas, and also in the hearts of those who knew and loved them.

Some years before Neilly passed away the twins took a trip to Thailand. Their quest was to find the grave of their Father's friend Duncan. At the time the girls had no idea in which cemetery Duncan had finally been buried. There were buses which ran to each war cemetery. The twins decided to board the bus heading for Kanchanaburi in Thailand, and joined an Australian group who were trying to find the grave of a relative. Arriving at the cemetery they were all able to consult a plan showing the names of those buried there, and the location of their graves. Sadly the Australian family were unable to find any trace of their relative, but Duncan McShane's name was there. The twins were delighted, and were at last able to visit their Father's friend's final resting place. Kathleen and Mary took photographs of the grave for their Father, and also for Duncan's relatives back in Helensburgh.

When Neilly was in his late seventies he was asked to attend a ceremony in Helensburgh to commemorate the 50th anniversary of Victory over the Japanese, and the lives of the soldiers and POW lost in the 2nd World War. Never fond of being in the lime light Neilly at first declined. Then after some thought on behalf of his lost friend Duncan and other comrades who had never come home, he accepted. On the day of the ceremony which was held in the town's Hermitage Park Neilly read out a speech he had prepared, and then planted a tree in memory of the men lost during that dreadful War. Overhead the Red Arrow pilots gave their salute from the sky.

I do not remember Duncan McShane. I was not yet born before he was gone. If I had been, I know I would have liked him so very, very much.

Duncan died at age 24 on the 12th of September 1943. His remains were eventually re-interred at Kanchanaburi War Cemetery Thailand.

The survivors

I do not think I ever met my second cousin Scrapper, although I do remember his daughters Susan and Elizabeth. Elizabeth is about my age and shares my name. When I was around sixteen or seventeen years old, over the school summer holidays, I worked in an old fashioned steam laundry across the road from our house. The last steam laundry in the land I think! I mainly worked in a small area with a number of different bits of equipment designed to dry and press shirts. Scrapper's elder daughter Susan had worked out that the last piece of equipment the shirts were put through also recorded the number processed. Susan also realised that by pressing and re-pressing the lever on this equipment the machine would continue to add to the total whether a shirt was inside or not. As we were all piece working, increasing the tally of the shirts finished, also increased our very meagre wages for the week. This became a daily practice. As soon as the manager, who was a nice little man, went out for his breaks the tally of finished shirts would speedily increase! The sisters today still live in Helensburgh. My Mother Patsy does have strong and fond memories of her first cousin who was the son of her mother's sister Susan.

Scrapper married Mary a lovely lady who sadly suffered years of poor health following a bad stroke at a fairly young age. She remembers that Scrapper was best man at Neilly and Rita's wedding. The couple were married on the 1st October 1946 in Saint Alphonsus Church Glasgow. Scrapper was also godfather to Neilly's first born son Johnnie. After leaving the army Scrapper worked in the building trade, being ganger on many jobs, notably with Mitchell Construction at the Faslane Naval Base when living quarters were being built in the late sixties and early seventies.

Scrapper often helped young lads find work and the twins remember he gave their brother Neil work as a labourer in Neil's student days during summer holidays. Neil remembers Scrapper as a hard but fair ganger. In earlier days as the owners of one of the first television sets in Kirkmichael estate, Mary and Scrapper had open house for kids to watch the telly. The McGinley boys loved these visits to watch their favourite children's programmes like the Lone Ranger, and Champion the Wonder Horse, whilst the twins enjoyed Captain Pugwash and Tom the Cabin Boy.

In later years Scrapper, having lost Mary who died in 1980, suffered failing health and failing sight. Nonetheless he still cut a dapper figure, with his distinctive white hat and smart walking stick, wandering along West Clyde Street promenade, or sitting on the sea wall, holding court with all who stopped for blether. Scrapper died in 1985 at the age of 69, and the town was all the poorer after the loss of this colourful character.

Company Commander Ernest Gordon was ordained as a minister on his return from the camp. David Boyle the officer who was tortured along with Neilly was awarded the Military Cross for his part in the Argylls campaign in Malaya. He also received the MBE for his POW work. He became Commandant at Erskine hospital in the city of Glasgow, which provides medical treatment and support facilities for service men.. Neilly and he did not meet again till many years after the war was over. Owenie Burke pursued a career as an antique dealer. As he soon became Neilly's brother in law Neilly saw him regularly throughout his life. Tragically Owenie died in a house fire in 1975 at aged 65.

Rita had been particularly close to her brother as her Mother had died when Rita was only fourteen and Owenie had been kind and caring to his Father and his youngest sister, paying for Rita's secondary education at the nearby Our Lady and St Francis School. An education which Rita greatly appreciated and one which stood her in good stead for the future.

Owenie's marriage to Chris a Dundee girl sadly did not last, and Owenie had returned to the family home at 5 Millroad St in Glasgow's Calton district to live with his Father and sister Rita. His older sister Katie and brother Nicky were now married and living elsewhere in the East End of Glasgow.

Efforts at marriage reconciliation failed and their son Terry was brought up by his Mother Chris. Many years later Terry became a doctor specialising in psychiatry and lived and worked in Singapore where his Father had many years earlier been a Japanese POW.

The tragic death of her dearest brother was heart breaking to Rita. It was also so very sad for Neilly who had lost his long time pal, and memories of their shared time in captivity must have flooded back. Neilly may have let his thoughts flow back to their cruel days in the Japanese camps, and his fall from the bridge. His friend in need already exhausted from his heavy long hours on the railway now carrying Neilly's weight, and shuffling bare foot in the night on the longest journey back to their prison camp. In the dark of the night both men suffered their own pain, yet in their struggle, both their hearts had beat as one.

In the late 1970's when Neilly lived in Kirkmichael in Helensburgh with his growing young family he helped start up a residents committee and a community centre was eventually built. Neilly although a simple brick layer, was a highly intelligent man. As a boy he was dux of his school. Nevertheless further education was not an option for the working class, and Neilly left school at fourteen years of age. His natural intelligence and his willing heart made him an ideal advisor to the people on the estate who trusted him. The residents brought their problems to Neilly who did his best to help those in need. The Kirkmichael community raised funds to provide facilities for the young people on the housing estate, and also for other deserving causes, one of which was for the patients at Erskine hospital. Neilly was asked to present the cheque in person. To his surprise and delight he met again David Boyle, his commander during his time in the P.O.W camps in Thailand, now in charge of Erskine Hospital

David Boyle gave a speech to the company gathered there, for the presentation. In the speech he praised Neilly's courage, and bravery in the camps, and said he was of the opinion, that the numbers of survivors of the camps would have been much smaller, if it hadn't been for the exploits and actions of a small gingered haired man who was present in the hall that evening! He spoke also of their torture together at the hands of the Japanese. These emotional words brought tears to Neilly's eyes and he remembered again all his comrades, young men and boys lost so long ago. Those like Duncan who had not returned to build new lives, marry have children and eventually grand children, as he had. Their deaths had been the ultimate sacrifice for they had given their lives for others. Neilly quietly recalled those other Helensburgh men like Willie Black a brother of Jeannie Galloway and father of Jean Black, who still lives in the town, who died on the 22nd February 1942 aged, 28. Willie was a POW in Pudu Gaol in Malaya, and now lies in Cheras War Cemetary in Malaya.
Jim Taylor survived the camps only to lose his life when a boat carrying him and other survivors was sunk by allies. When the camps were liberated the Japanese put those POW who did not need hospital treatment into unmarked boats which were often shelled by mistake by the allies. James Cruickshank who died on the 4th August 1943 aged 26 a POW in Thailand, now buried at

Kanchanaburi War Cemetary in Thailand. Neilly also thought of the POW from the Argylls who made it safely back to Helensburgh after the war. Ned Killen, Peter McKell, Jim Jardine, and Neil (Scrapper) Sharkey.

Closing my eyes for a moment, I can still hear Neilly singing the beautiful song he frequently sang at family gatherings. I now feel that this would be a fitting tribute and last farewell to Duncan McShane, and the other men who never returned home.

The Moon Is Shining O'er Malaya
Palm trees are swaying in the moonlight
Casting their shadows o'er the sea
What then will greet us in the morning
Just stay a while and listen here to me.

For the moon is shining o'er Malaya
And the stars twinkle down from up above
Girls in their sarongs and kabayas
In their kampongs as they sing their songs of love.

You can hear Terang Bulan and old Sarino
Songs their mothers sang in days gone by
From Penang to Ipoh and Malacca
You can hear those sweet enchanting lullabies.

For the guitars are strumming in the moonlight
And the echo of those kronchongs never dies
There's a moon shining brightly o'er Malaya
And to think we'll have to leave it bye and bye.

It is believed that the words of the song were written by two Argyll soldiers, Corporal James Greig and Bandsman Reg Taylor, and were sung to the tune of a popular romantic Malay song called Terang Bulan, the Perak State national anthem. Sadly both men later died in POW captivity, James Greig in Thailand, and Reg Taylor in Singapore.

Despite the torture near starvation and life threatening illnesses, Neilly suffered during his years in the Thai and Malay camps, working on Death Railway, Neilly in later years was not bitter. He had had, the most wonderful life, with his lovely wife Rita. Together they created a wonderful family.

For me, I don't know quite, how to end this book. I cannot let it go. Still someone unseen seems to be standing behind me, nudging me gently to the pull of the clock, for it is now time to go. Yet as long as I live, I will always remember Neilly, my dearest Uncle, with his laughing blue eyes, and his beautiful unspoilt heart.

Neilly in his Argyll and Southern Highlanders dress uniform age 20

After the war Neilly with his father John and mother Mary pictured in Ireland

Neilly and his cousin "Scrapper" (Neil Sharkey) 1n 1945.

Neilly and Rita in their Golden Years

The Three Amigos Neilly and two workmates on a building project

Grandmother McGinley with some of her grandchildren on her 80th birthday

Neilly with his boys   Johnie, Michael, Neil, Gerard, Owen, Pat, and Hugh

Elizabeth and brother Terence
on holiday in Ireland

Elizabeth in Ireland

Neilly planting the tree on VJ day in memory of Duncan and the other Prisoners of War who never returned home

Neilly making a heartfelt speech at the planting ceremony

Neilly and Rita and their extended family pictured in St Josephs Church Helensburgh